COVID-19 and Ethics in Canada

The Failure of Common Decency

JON PARSONS

HCE PRESS

HCE Press
Toronto, ON, Canada

COVID-19 and Ethics in Canada: The Failure of Common Decency / Jon Parsons

Print ISBN: 978-0-9953350-4-2
EBook ISBN: 978-0-9953350-5-9

To everyone who tried.

There's no question of heroism in all this. It's a matter of common decency. That's an idea which may make some people smile, but the only means of fighting a plague is common decency.

Albert Camus, The Plague

Table of Contents

Introduction

The first two years of the COVID-19 pandemic in Canada stretched from March 2020 to March 2022. In that time, it claimed the lives of more than 37,000 people in the country, though there are indications the actual number could be much higher.[1] Public discussions of the pandemic often focus on hard data. What people hear in news stories and statements from public officials is mostly scientific and technical. Voices and forms of knowledge that go unheard are those of humanists, philosophers, and social scientists.

COVID-19 is a term that indicates a biological organism – a virus. Epidemiology and mathematical modelling explain its spread and function in the world. Medical practitioners speak to its impacts on the human body and on the population at a community level. Statisticians depict the results in tables, charts, and graphs.

But COVID-19 is also a social and cultural phenomenon. It changed the way of life for people in Canada and around the world. It changed how people work and interact. It changed elements of the consumer economy and the things people do

---

[1] Research on excess deaths, comparing the COVID-19 era with any typical years, shows the death toll could be double the official figure. See Tara Moriarty et al., "Excess all-cause mortality during the COVID-19 epidemic in Canada," Royal Society of Canada, 2021.

for entertainment. And almost overnight, it changed what was considered appropriate behaviour in public and the meaning of right and wrong. The pandemic has been, from the outset, about ways of living and ways of acting, and therefore fundamentally about ethics.

While objective facts cannot fully represent complex human life, that is not to say data has no value or cannot inform ethical action. Case numbers, for example, can justify lockdowns and point to the correct moral choice. But starting from ethical action is a different motivation than simply doing what the data says. My view since the beginning of the pandemic, and still my view now, is that basing action on ethics is a better motivation and yields better results. The reasons people act are sometimes as important as the actions themselves.

Beginning in March of 2020, I set out to intervene in the public discussion by writing about the pandemic from the point of view of ethics. I wrote brief essays and articles on significant flashpoints to do with COVID-19 in Canada. Along with writing journalism, I have an academic background, and ethics is, of course, a philosophical subject. But I did not want these writings to be academic as such. Instead, I tried to write accessible prose and create content people could read quickly and then apply in their everyday lives.

Ricochet, an independent Canadian media outlet, published most of the early chapters that make up this book. I wrote a series of some ten articles for this outlet called "Ethics in an era of COVID-19." *The Independent NL*, a media outlet in my home province of Newfoundland and Labrador, published some of the other articles that came to be chapters in this book. I wrote a few chapters as white papers or briefs and have not published them before.

The book is organized in chronological order, tracking the pandemic over two years. I made only minor changes to the early chapters, as I am interested in maintaining something of a record of the issues as they came up and the experience of the pandemic as it unfolded. I annotated the chapters, often to make some retrospective comment or to give an update with new information that came to light since the original publication.

Each chapter takes up an issue or concept related to the pandemic with an ethical dimension. Examples include social solidarity, collective values as opposed to individual values, vaccines and anti-vaccine protests, panic-buying and hoarding, governance and decision-making, and the duty we have as individuals, communities, and a country to care for others. Along with the focus on ethics, a number of chapters discuss unrest and take up positions on protest and contentious politics, which relates to my ongoing work in the field of resistance studies, my main academic area. Some chapters discuss the pandemic as a looking-glass, showing cracks and divisions that existed in Canadian society and that were brought to light all the more vividly and magnified in a time of crisis. Examples include inequalities and injustices of class, race, gender, and disability, among others.

Along similar lines as this idea of the pandemic as a looking-glass, the novelist and political activist Arundhati Roy published an article in April 2020 describing the pandemic as a portal. She notes:

Historically, pandemics have forced humans to break with the past and imagine their world anew. This one is no different. It is a portal, a gateway between one world and the next. We can choose to walk through it, dragging the carcasses of our prejudice and hatred, our avarice, our data banks and dead ideas, our dead rivers and smoky skies behind us. Or we can walk through lightly, with little luggage, ready to imagine another world. And ready to fight for it.[2]

I initially thought the pandemic, while a severe crisis heralding an era of disruption, was also an opportunity for significant change. I thought it was a moment when people would step up, come together, and enact the best values toward collective well-being. As a long-time activist and community organizer, I always thought people had it within themselves to rise to moments of significant challenge and find ways to overcome.

To be sure, there were some moments when it seemed like people were coming together to face adversity as a common front. There was a great deal of initial vim for social solidarity, even if it was going by other terminology, in the first weeks of the outbreak in Canada, when the entire country went into lockdown. People found ways to support one another. There was an explosion of mutual-aid networking. People were singing their support from the rooftops and cheering for healthcare workers. It was a moment of deep uncertainty, but it was also a moment of shared struggle. I discuss forms of social solidarity in the first chapter in the collection, "COVID-19 outbreak calls for an ethics of collective care."

But that all stopped and quicker than I would have imagined. Issues came up with financial support for workers and expectations for those whose work was called essential. There emerged forms of racism and stigma aimed at specific communities and related to the borders. With global shortages of personal protective equipment and other goods necessary for dealing with the pandemic, there was also a tendency toward nationalism and xenophobia. Then, by the end of 2020 and the beginning of 2021, it became clear what was happening was a

---

[2] Arundhati Roy's widely syndicated article, "The pandemic is a portal," first published in *FT*, April 3, 2020.

profound failure of ethical action and common decency. As Roy would have it, we dragged the carcasses of our dead ideas through the portal with us.

The trajectory of the argument weaving its way through this book moves from believing in the potential for ethical action, to recognizing the failure of ethical action, and then finally to attempting to understand that failure and its implications.

I want to be clear that recognizing this failure of ethical action is not any statement on human nature. It is not to say that people are fundamentally incapable in this regard, but that the conditions did not exist for widespread and collectively oriented ethical action to happen in this place and time. I also want to be clear that there is a great deal of regional variation in Canada. I do not mean to disparage places like my home province of Newfoundland and Labrador, which was a beacon for a time of just the kinds of collective values and social solidarity that would have made a difference across the country.[3]

Some of the chapters below focus specifically on qualifying this failure of ethical action. I direct interested readers to "What explains the Canadian failure on COVID-19?" and "The failure of common decency." The second of these pieces takes a perspective on ethical failure in line with Camus' analysis in *The Plague*. But whereas in that book Camus concluded there was a fundamental human decency in the response to an outbreak of plague, my analysis sees a failure of common decency.

Later chapters of the book attempt to think through the context of the so-called reopening of society and learning to

---

[3] On this point, numerous studies show that places with higher degrees of social cohesion fared better in the pandemic. See for example Rae L. Jewett et al., "Social cohesion and community resilience during COVID-19 and pandemics," *International Journal of Health Services* 51.3, 2021; and James B. Davies, "Economic inequality and COVID-19 deaths and cases in the first wave: A cross-country analysis," *Canadian Public Policy* 47.4, 2021.

live with the virus. Having decided that the effort to contain the virus is too great, public officials created a situation where people act as individuals who look after themselves first, further diminishing the possibility of cultivating ethical action by invalidating confidence in the collective. Telling people to manage their own risks and make their own choices, paired with the abandonment of all public health measures, increases the risks and marginalization of vulnerable people. The individual management of a public health crisis is not only absurd but effectively prohibits ethical action, in the sense that people are compelled to act in ways that endanger and restrict the choices of vulnerable people.

Concerning where things go from here, there is, in my view, a serious reckoning to be made for what has happened. I am not confident many people in this country will be anxious to truly engage with the scale of failure and human tragedy that is our legacy from the pandemic. It may have long-term impacts on social relations, workplaces, families, and on the very idea of what it means to be Canadian. Such a failure also raises questions about challenges coming in the future, such as the capacity to deal with the consequences of climate change. An article by Lucian Ashworth in *The Independent NL* points out that compared to the entirely predictable disruptions coming in the decades ahead because of climate change, the pandemic is the same as a tutorial level in a video game – this is the easy part.[4] Given how Canada responded to the pandemic, I find it difficult to imagine, as things currently stand, this country could adequately rise to the challenges that are coming.

This is typically when the writer is obliged to offer some redemptive move and say things can still work out for the

---

[4] Lucian Ashworth, "Thinking outside the crisis: A tutorial level in apocalypse(s)," *The Independent NL*, April 24, 2020.

best. I suppose I can say, to reiterate, that I do not believe there is anything fundamental about human nature that caused such a failure of ethical action and it is possible something could happen to inspire widespread change. But the experience of the pandemic has been, at least for me, a source of enormous disappointment. That disappointment is not entirely irredeemable, but I will not be putting a positive spin on things at the close of the book or saying everything will be okay. If you are the type of reader who needs that, perhaps it is best to part ways here. But if you are the type of reader who wants to peer through the looking-glass and try to account for what has happened in Canada in the COVID-19 pandemic, then read on.

A word on ethics

As mentioned above, I did not set out to write academic essays but rather to write accessible prose for a public audience. Still, I want to make some brief comments on the main theoretical underpinnings of the chapters and how I understand ethics. Even if left unsaid in favour of plain language and journalistic tone, the collection does have an underlying set of principles and conventions for ethical action.

When people think of ethics, they intuitively understand it to be about right and wrong. Along with the characteristics of what it means to be a good person and live a good life, ethics is also something people understand as especially relevant for some professions, like doctors and lawyers. However, when a discussion of ethics turns to something that people live with on a day-to-day basis, like ethical action in a pandemic, it can take on connotations of blame and shame.

For example, many people will feel that giving to charity is a measure of ethical behaviour. So too is supporting the right causes and having views that align with noble principles of social justice. It is also about buying the right products and being the kind of person who volunteers. Most people like to think of themselves as being essentially good and feel, even if unconsciously, some pressure to adhere to a set of conventions for what it means to be good. When people encounter things that challenge their view of themselves as essentially good, it can be highly uncomfortable. And so, any ethical discussions of issues in the public sphere can be perceived as antagonistic and shaming. Anyone who discusses such matters can then be seen as acting morally superior, or as so-called virtue signalling.

Unfortunately, some of this is unavoidable when speaking about ethics in public, as it will inevitably make some people feel uncomfortable. It is not a stretch to say that asking difficult questions and making people uncomfortable is at the origin of ethical philosophy. But even so, ethics is not, in point of fact, about who is a better person or who can claim the purest moral stand. Instead, it is about recognizing the faults in the taken-for-granted ways our society functions and how that impacts our choices and actions.

When thinking about public ethics, it is also essential that there is no separation between the one who is doing the analysis and the public they are analyzing. The ethicist is, in this sense, one of the people and not apart from them, and just like the public, the ethicist is by no means perfect. For example, just because I am interested in trying to understand what it means to act decently in the context of a pandemic does not mean that I did everything right or that I consider myself to be better than anyone else. Moreover, to engage in ethical analysis is always to criticize oneself first, and then to be willing to dwell on the discomfort that may cause. This notion is nicely encapsulated in the popular set of Scandinavian social conventions known as *Jantelagen*, which are a prohibition against setting oneself apart from other people, whether with respect to wealth or righteousness, with the directive "you are not to see yourself as better than us."[5] The ethicist is not sitting in judgement of others and is simply another imperfect human being attempting to make sense of the world.

Ethics in the public sphere is, in this sense, a form of applied ethics. It is not a thought experiment of people tied to railroad tracks, and it is not about ideal societies or the ultimate form of the good. It is about taking a problem or issue people are dealing with in the world and then understanding or solving it through ethically oriented practices. To put forward a set of ethically oriented practices is, of course, to recommend what it means to be good. Applied ethics always relies on overarching principles and a specific approach that informs ethical action. A recommendation for what constitutes ethical action and the ethical person is just that – a recommendation. No one is obliged to agree with any particular set of ethical principles.

My conception of the ethical subject related to the COVID-19 pandemic draws from the work of Simon Critchley and the ethics of commitment he formulated in *Infinitely Demanding*.[6] Much of Critchley's wide-ranging work on ethics has a decidedly activist perspective, as he seeks a form of ethical subject that enables authentic political and social change. A helpful way to understand Critchley's ethical subject and the ethics of commitment is by juxtaposing it with two types of nihilistic subjectivity: passive nihilism and active nihilism.

Passive nihilism describes a subjectivity that perceives the world around them in chaos and, in response, then makes the decision to turn inwards and focus on themselves. The passive nihilist does not attempt to change what is wrong in the world, either because it seems too daunting or dangerous to

---

[5] These social conventions are from the novel by Aksel Sandemose, *A Fugitive Crosses His Tracks*, 1933.

[6] Simon Critchley, *Infinitely Demanding: Ethics of Commitment, Politics of Resistance*, Verso, 2013.

confront, and instead chooses hedonism or whatever will make them happiest at the immediate moment. In the context of the pandemic, the passive nihilist wants their creature comforts. They miss most of all their haircuts and going out to brunch. They want to go on holiday amid suffering and disease.

A second type of nihilistic subjectivity that can be juxtaposed with the ethics of commitment is active nihilism. Whereas passive nihilism indicates a turning inward, active nihilism is about lashing out. It describes a subjectivity that sees the world in chaos and, in response, decides to make that world more chaotic still. They do not attempt to change the world because they see that changing things is too daunting a task. Out of frustration with their inability to do anything about the problems around them, they choose to burn the world to the ground. In the context of the pandemic, the active nihilist is the person who fights against any reasonable attempts to contain the virus. They are against lockdowns, against masks, against vaccines, and against anyone who tries to keep others safe. They insist on breaking any rules put in place and do so in a way that is always brash. They set up protests at hospitals and grocery stores and generally attempt to sabotage any formal or informal organizations that try to help.

These two nihilistic subjectivities are, of course, something of a caricature. However, I am sure many will identify a few people who perfectly fit the descriptions. It is also the case that people are not one thing consistently and forever. People shift in their actions and motivations. But even as these are generalizations, they describe broad trends and attitudes that have been easy to see throughout the pandemic. These two nihilisms rightly perceive the world around them in chaos and recognize there is little anyone can do to fix the situation.

The ethical subject is different from both passive and active nihilists but recognizes the same things. They perceive the world in chaos and know that no adequate response will fix the situation. But whereas passive and active nihilists are resigned to that fate and fall into patterns of either hedonism or lashing out, the ethical subject recognizes its inability to fix things but tries anyway. The ethical subject is formed in relation to an unfulfillable demand – thus Critchley's "infinitely demanding." In the context of the pandemic, they understand it is an unfair situation, and they know it is not in their power to make the virus go away. Still, they commit to doing whatever they can to minimize the suffering of others. As opposed to the nihilistic subjectivities, they are not entirely focused on themselves as individuals but try to think about what is best for the collective well-being of their community. The ethical subject makes a commitment to social solidarity even while recognizing there is some absurdity to it, in the sense that they know their actions will make little difference in the face of such tragedy. They simply cannot help but try.

I use this ethical subject and ethics of commitment as my vantage point for the analysis and discussion in the chapters to follow. I want to stress again that this is not about blame or shame. I do not think people are at fault for falling into passive or active nihilism, and I do not believe that people who find themselves compelled to act as ethical subjects are heroes. These were all people facing a chaotic and challenging situation, and they all did what seemed best in their own life and context. In the end, as I argue, it was not enough to avert tragedy and failure, but that does not mean we all cannot do better the next time there is a critical situation, another pandemic or some other crisis, and there will be a next time.

COVID-19 outbreak calls for an ethics of collective care

Individual panic and efforts at self-preservation need to give way to caring for people we have never met

Canadians are waiting for a major coronavirus outbreak that seems all but certain.[1] Exactly how it will unfold, which regions will be most affected, and the potential human toll remain the subjects of speculation, but no one doubts that a difficult time is at hand.

Much of the discussion about the virus centres on numbers and data, such as how many will get sick, what age groups will be most affected, mortality rates, economic impacts, and so on. There are a range of numbers and data for all this, even as much is uncertain. My intent in writing this series is to discuss the COVID-19 crisis from the point of view of ethics. It is not to say the numbers do not matter, since, of course, numbers will inform this ethical discussion in significant ways, at least in the sense that statistics and data are a primary form of information

---

[1] Published in *Ricochet*, March 16, 2020, this article was the first in the series of articles, which were published under a column titled "Ethics in an era of COVID-19." The WHO declared the pandemic on March 11, 2020.

for understanding what is happening with respect to the spread of the virus. But while so much of the public discussion is focused on numbers, my perspective is cultural and philosophical.

Collectivism vs. individualism

The most obvious ethical dimension of the virus outbreak is the way it calls on us, as communities and as residents of this country, to enact altruism for the collective good.

For example, individuals are enacting a range of health strategies such as increased hand-washing, not touching their face, staying at home if they are sick, and avoiding large gatherings, among other measures.[2] Other strategies include social distancing, self-isolation, and quarantining.

In the first instance, these are things that individuals can do to avoid personally getting infected. In a general sense, the thinking that motivates these behaviours is often focused on the self – "others may get infected but I will not." A related type of self-centred thinking is what motivates hoarding and panic-buying – "I must stockpile resources to keep myself safe."

To be clear, by "hoarding" I do not mean putting away a few extra non-perishable food items or preparing to be isolated at

---

[2] At this point in the early days of the pandemic, there was still uncertainty about the way the virus was being transmitted, with hand-washing and surface disinfection, even disinfecting groceries, being a focus for many. It would take a long time for messaging from health authorities to come around to the fact that the virus was airborne and transmitted mostly by both droplets and aerosols, with some not even recognizing this fact up to today. In retrospect, many precautions visible in public, like arrows marking the direction for shoppers to walk in stores or spacing lines marked to show two metres, and even the proliferation of hand sanitizer being made available in public, were merely a form of hygiene theatre, even though such measures may have inspired some degree of confidence for people trying to make sense of an evolving situation.

home for a couple of weeks. Stocking up on necessary and essential items is part of being responsible and part of moral action at this time. By "hoarding" I mean the types of behaviour that clearly go beyond the pale, such as buying thousands of dollars' worth of disinfectants or toilet paper or surgical masks.[3]

The self-centred perspective of the world as a battle of all against all obviously predates this recent coronavirus outbreak. Individuals are pitted against one another in competition over apparently limited economic and material resources, and hoarding behaviour and panic-buying are the day-to-day business of banks and of markets and of speculation.

However, the main reason health authorities are encouraging people to practice good hygiene and to get prepared for possible quarantines by stocking up is not simply so that individuals can protect themselves. Yes, it is true that people can and should try their best to avoid becoming infected, and people should certainly try to enact recommended health and preparation strategies. However, the reason for doing so is not about keeping isolated individuals safe. It is to give the healthcare system a fighting chance to deal with the outbreak in a manageable way, rather than in an overwhelming flood of cases.[4]

Flattening the curve

In short, the reason it is important for everyone to do their best to avoid becoming infected is not just about their own self-preservation. It is, in a much more significant sense, actually

---

[3] Scenes of panic-buying in grocery stores and other retail outlets were common, with toilet paper an item that was in demand. Price gouging on items like hand sanitizer was common.

[4] The notion of flattening the curve, used by health officials, was in many ways a call for social solidarity, though the language used by government officials was typically more along the lines of "doing your part," rather than explicitly using the term solidarity.

about preserving the well-being of the collective and those most vulnerable to the worst effects of the virus.

So, for example, if a significant proportion of the population is most likely going to become infected over the lifespan of this pandemic no matter what, it is important this does not happen all at once, since the healthcare system does not have capacity to deal with all the serious cases at the same time. As communities and as residents of this country, we need to work together to slow the spread of the virus such that the healthcare system can cope. The same number of people may well become infected, but over a longer time frame, so the outcomes for the most vulnerable people are better.

The shift in thinking here is from a self-centred to a collective perspective. It is a call to act in ways that account for people we have never met. It is a call for a kind of altruism and collective ethics that are in many ways the opposite of the typical "me against the world" mentality. If only one person washes their hands, it makes little difference whatsoever to anyone except for that one person. But millions of people enacting good health practices can make an enormous difference. This is the idea of collective care.

Motivation matters

The move to a collectivist ethics to frame our response to the coronavirus outbreak impacts individual motives for action. It gives us a different reason to do many of the same things we may already be doing to keep ourselves from getting infected. But in this perspective the motivation is a collective-oriented altruism rather than a more typical self-centredness. It is a call for all of us to care for one another.

Perhaps collective attitudes are a way to avoid some of the panic and hoarding that may grip a worried population, because from this view the reason for action is not only rooted in self-preservation. In a situation of crisis, we are called to behave in ways that take into account the well-being of others, called to participate in a worthy effort that is larger than ourselves. And so hoarding, for example, is highly unethical. Likewise, altruism and acting toward common or collective goals is a much better motivation for action, and one that will lead to better outcomes, than purely self-centred or individual motivation.

A bartender's perspective: COVID-19 and precarious workers

As businesses throughout Canada close, a whole underclass of workers face uncertainty

Along with my employment as a writer and researcher, I work part-time as a bartender in Toronto.[1] The bar I work at is more of a neighbourhood pub, and in the regular course of business I generally enjoy the interactions with the customers. It is not a bad gig at all.

But this last week, as the World Health Organization declared the new coronavirus a pandemic, as reported infections more than doubled in Ontario, and as senior government officials and celebrities went into isolation, customers came into the bar who were coughing and obviously sick. I was furious about this, but I wasn't exactly in any position to say anything because, as you know, the customer is always right. Of course, there is no reason to assume they were infected with the virus, but then again there

---

[1] Published in *Ricochet*, March 17, 2020. At that time, there was little clarity whether there would be any kind of financial assistance in place for all the precarious workers who would be put out of work by the lockdown, and there was a great deal of anxiety about this among service industry workers.

is no reason to assume they were not. Just by being in the bar, they were taking liberties with the health and safety of the staff and all the other customers.[2]

As I thought about this, I realized it was totally irresponsible. It was irresponsible of the customers who were sick for being out in public. But it was also irresponsible of me for the part I played in facilitating social gatherings at a time when social distancing was necessary. I also realized it was why, in due course, all the bars and restaurants in Toronto would need to be shut down. And in fact, the Ontario government did recently order all bars closed to help limit the spread of the virus.[3]

Precarious workers need support and respect

But what does this mean for all the service industry workers who are now without an income? As businesses throughout Canada close, a whole underclass of workers will be affected and face uncertainty: cleaners, grocery store workers, gym workers, housekeepers, retail workers, cooks and dishwashers, daycare workers, undocumented workers and migrants, delivery drivers, gig workers, and many others – all the working people who are paid minimum wage or less, who work part-time, with no job security, no benefits or sick days, and who are essentially held hostage by economic necessity to risk their health and the health of their families.

Over the last couple of days, the federal and provincial governments have been making announcements on some financial

---

[2] It will be interesting to see what the tolerance will be for people deciding to go out in public when they are obviously ill in the aftermath of the pandemic, as the behavior was so common before as to be unremarkable.

[3] The order from the Ontario provincial government to close all service industry, gyms, and other venues actually came as this article was with the editors, and the sentence about the closures had to be added on the day of publication.

help for Canadians. I can understand that there are lots of moving pieces, but it has all been extremely vague. Whereas there has been at least some clarity for middle-class and working-class people with respect to employment insurance benefits, any assistance remains totally unclear for the precarious underclass. The first concern for broader Canadian society right now is health. Precarious workers are going to get sick and are not going to be able to take time off. It is easy to imagine how dangerous that is.

The inequality epidemic

But in a more general sense this emergency situation is simply highlighting an ongoing ethical wrong in our country, one that has not been addressed, and rarely acknowledged, all along. The inequality and precariousness that exists in Canada is an epidemic on its own. Now the social epidemic is brought to light by the biological epidemic, and one reinforces and spurs the other. Not just the government but Canadian society at large needs to step up and find or demand solutions for the underclass. Solutions need to be clear, unequivocal, and easy to access. This needs to happen now.[4]

Proponents of a universal basic income will likely find little solace in being able to now say "we told you so." But as a solution, a universal basic income would be an immediate stopgap against financial calamity and would, by extension, contribute in a significant way to addressing the impacts of COVID-19 on the healthcare system.

---

[4] The solution that ended up coming from the federal government was the Canadian Emergency Response Benefit (CERB) and later an expansion and extension of employment insurance benefits. There was also a benefits program in place on the employer side, the COVID Wage Subsidy, to allow workplaces to keep employees on the payroll even if their operations were limited. A great deal of this employer subsidy was given to the largest corporations in the country.

Whatever the solution is, this is a conversation that needs to happen now, as major sectors of the commercial economy shut down and as more and more already precarious workers find themselves in an even worse predicament. So, while this pandemic is an urgent and multifaceted crisis, it is also an opportunity to examine how inequality functions in Canada and find ways to fix that for good.

COVID-19 has exposed society's upside-down priorities

The pandemic is teaching us about what matters and what has been possible all along

Before anything else, I want to acknowledge what is unfolding in Canada and around the globe as a human tragedy.[1] Even as this crisis offers an object lesson and has things to teach us, it is important to never lose sight of the scale of calamity in terms of suffering and loss of life.

Just in the last week all the rules have changed and Canada has been turned upside down. Of course, our country is just now coming to grips with the same form of crisis other regions have been grappling with for weeks or months, and that the entire world will be dealing with for the foreseeable future. But as the world is swiftly changing and the country is turned upside down, some things are also becoming abundantly clear. The pandemic is a looking-glass. It is providing us with an object lesson, with a practical means of learning something important and essential about our country and about the world.

This object lesson has several aspects, and it will continue to reveal more aspects as the crisis unfolds. Here in the early days,

---

[1] Published in *Ricochet*, March 19, 2020.

I want to briefly discuss just a few that seem to me immediately obvious: 1) what has always been essential, 2) the experience of insecurity, and 3) what has always been possible.

What is essential

As the social and economic life of Canada grinds to a halt, there are some things we can clearly do without, and some things that are absolutely essential. Simply think about what work *must* continue to be done and what work can be put aside.

There is no need to create a hierarchy of essential work, but it is clear that in the present crisis healthcare workers and all forms of activity that support health care are absolutely vital. Support for workers in health care, both material and emotional, needs to be a major priority going forward.

Along with workers in healthcare, work in food production and distribution is absolutely vital. It is so plain and obvious that communities need a reliable supply of food to survive, but it is also something that is typically taken for granted, and only comes to light as vital in a time of crisis.[2] Agricultural workers (a significant number of whom are migrants and sometimes undocumented), truck drivers, warehouse workers, and grocery store and shop employees are all absolutely essential.

Then there are also essential people like cleaners, sanitation workers, utility workers in electricity and water and sewage, childcare providers, postal workers, delivery drivers, and a range of other workers who allow life in a state of emergency to continue. This work supports the basic existence of millions every day, and all these workers are taking risks with their health and the health of their families so that life continues.

---

[2] Part of the reason for the panic-buying that punctuated the early weeks of the outbreak in Canada was, arguably, tied to this recognition of the potential scarcity of food or severe disruption of distribution networks.

I would also add, though perhaps not in the same category of vital but still in my opinion essential, all the artists and creatives who have produced the cultural products that so many now consume while secluded in their homes. People need more than to simply feed the body. Especially in times of crisis, they also need to feed the soul.

I am not going to list the range of occupations that do not come close to being essential. It is straightforward enough to simply think about all those things that make little difference to human well-being at this time. Though it should be said that these are the occupations and sectors that tend to be the most privileged and highest paid in the "normal" times before the rules changed. Ironically, many of the workers who are essential are the very people who have been the targets of round upon round of austerity and belt-tightening by provincial and federal governments for decades, whereas many of those who are less than essential have been the beneficiaries of round upon round of largess.

The experience of insecurity

The new "normal" for the foreseeable future is uncertainty. No one knows what might happen in a month or two, and it is not difficult to imagine the rules that have changed so radically in just a matter of weeks will change even more. People are losing their jobs, their savings, and their investments. People can no longer carry out everyday activities or leisure, and even simple but necessary activities like getting food require planning and caution. This is the experience of insecurity.

Some commentators and politicians liken the situation to wartime. Canadians, for the most part, have little experience with the insecurity associated with war, but it is easier to imagine how difficult life in conflict must be from what we have experienced just for a few days. It is easier to imagine the impossible decisions so many refugees of conflict must face, how terrifying it must be to shelter against the possibility of bombings, drones, and bullets. The threat we in Canada now face by comparison might be called benign.

But along with teaching us something of the insecurity that people in war-torn countries experience, this crisis also teaches us about the insecurity that so many people inside Canada have faced for so long. It teaches us something of the experience of those in poverty or who are experiencing homelessness, those who are marginalized, those who are disabled, and those who are traumatized or subject to forms of physical or systemic violence. Insecurity exists in many forms in this country. And now that insecurity is the experience of the majority, it is even worse again for those who have experienced insecurity all along. The vulnerable are even more vulnerable now.[3]

Insecurity means that everything becomes difficult. It causes stress, anxiety, and panic. It means that the taken-for-granted, simple, everyday things that were easy yesterday may become impossible tomorrow. And as a general and widespread form of insecurity becomes the new "normal," we are called as neighbours and communities to care for one another, especially the most vulnerable.

What is possible

Along with these pandemic lessons about what is essential and what insecurity means, the COVID-19 crisis is also teaching us about what has been possible all along. For example, just in the last few days, federal and provincial governments have found the money to enact far-reaching measures to address the crisis.

---

[3] As I discuss in later chapters, it is precisely these most vulnerable people, who were made even more vulnerable by the pandemic, who experienced some of the worst outcomes of increasing insecurity and neglect.

There are hastily arranged and enormous financial packages, suspension of evictions, programs for people experiencing homelessness, and presumably even more elaborate schemes as the days and weeks go by. The federal government has proclaimed it will deploy some of the massive "fiscal firepower" at its disposal to help ordinary people in unprecedented ways.

Obviously this was something that could have happened all along. The system was always in a position to do something about the yawning inequality and injustice in the country. It was always possible to help the vulnerable and downtrodden. It was always possible that things could have been better for everyone. But that is not the way the world before was. The country was, in the days before the crisis, punctuated by greed and hoarding on a massive scale. Selfishness was prized and awarded bonuses, even as working people were told to tighten their belts and to do without, and even as social security and programs for collective well-being were gutted.

Let us never lose sight of this unfolding tragedy as first of all a tragedy of human suffering. But let us also learn the lessons this crisis has to offer. Let us look with a clear vision at what has always been essential and what has always been possible. And as the old world crumbles let us build something better, something fair, and something that addresses, for good, the insecurity that has plagued our country for so long.

Why are so many not following COVID-19 guidelines?

People who have never been shown social solidarity are ill-equipped to enact it

Over the last week, a number of stories appeared in the media highlighting people not following physical distancing and quarantine protocols for COVID-19.[1] In Vancouver, hordes of people decided to get out on the weekend and enjoy the warm weather. In Corner Brook, Newfoundland, the same person was arrested twice for breaking an order to self-isolate. And a person in Quebec City who tested positive for COVID-19 and was told to self-isolate instead went for a stroll around the neighbourhood. In Toronto, ridership on the TTC was down 50%, but cars still clogged the streets, families went to the parks, and friends got together for parties.[2] In fact, a recent Abacus poll showed a frightening number of people admit they are not adhering to physical distancing practices: 12% say they are not

---

[1] Published in *Ricochet*, April 4, 2020.

[2] Toronto Transit Commission data was something I followed in the early weeks of the pandemic to get some sense of how the city was responding to the lockdown. By the end of March 2020, ridership was down almost 75%. As time went on, TTC data was highly instructive in showing which neighbourhoods had more workers in essential jobs and who could and could not afford to self-isolate.

avoiding crowded public places (3.6 million), 19% are not refraining from touching objects in public (5.7 million), and 30% (9 million) are not refraining from getting together with family.[3]

This is not to say that only a few people are taking COVID-19 protocols seriously, and the data shows that most people in fact are. Many individuals have not left home at all for the last few weeks and are ready to stay in self-isolation for as long as it takes. But if staying home except for essential trips out is required of everyone right now, why are so many people, even if a minority, not taking this seriously?

Patterns of behaviour

There is a tendency among pundits to attribute anti-social and in this case dangerous behaviours to pure stupidity or to say it is the action of a "few bad apples." This is on display in the Twitter hashtag #COVIDIOTS, in which people post images or anecdotes to shame those not practicing physical distancing.[4] But while shame and ostracism have some power to compel better behaviour, attributing anti-social attitudes to simple stupidity misses the root causes and limits buy-in for collective efforts. And, unfortunately, it also provides clear justification for authoritarian and draconian approaches to enforcement.

In our society, people have been taught particular patterns of behaviour and attitudes that get in the way of social solidarity. The often-unspoken rules for how the world works and what is considered appropriate can come back to haunt communities when, during times of crisis, they need collectivist attitudes.

---

[3] See the report from Abacus Data, "National Survey on COVID-19," March 22, 2020.

[4] Along with being a term that makes no attempt to understand the underlying causes of the behaviours it critiques, it is also an example of ableist language.

Ask yourself, for example, the following questions around issues that may come up as impediments to social solidarity.

Is it surprising that millennials, many of whom have been cast into precarious living and working conditions, have never had the benefits of unionized employment, and have seen their social security net dismantled, might express some cynicism at the call to participate in a collectivist project of social solidarity?

Is it surprising that baby boomers, many of whom have been handed every benefit and shielded from any harm for decades, might assume this current crisis cannot touch them?

Or is it at all surprising that a society predicated on the idea that a small number of powerful people are allowed to take liberties with the safety and security of everyone else might not be well equipped to enact widespread collective care?

Is it surprising that within a political culture that tells people the limit of their involvement is voting every four years, and in which grassroots politics is all too often written off as virtue signalling, might not be the best for mobilizing a population?

Is it surprising that telling people to stay at home and also telling people in some trades to keep going to non-essential work might cause dissonance and skepticism?[5]

And is it surprising at all that people might distrust governments and institutions of all kinds when those same institutions are often a source of harm for migrants, people experiencing homelessness, people with addictions, and other marginalized people?

---

[5] Here, I was thinking specifically of Ontario premier Doug Ford's decision to categorize construction projects as essential work, and to eventually institute laws to extend construction hours. It was a choice to accommodate a group of developers and a particular industry ahead of the well-being of the population, in the sense that people were already obliged to spend more time at home, or even working from home, and then had to listen to construction noise while they were there.

What to do next

These rhetorical questions are based at least in part on some generalizations and oversimplifications. But what I am gesturing toward are a few of the socially oriented reasons Canada is ill-prepared for a crisis like this and why significant numbers of people are not taking seriously their ethical duty of collective care. Still, pointing these things out is not a solution, and it seems that a solution of some kind is required.

The solution that the government will likely take, based on the widespread idea that stupid behaviour by the bad apples needs to be stopped, will be an authoritarian approach. Some examples of this that are already in operation are snitch lines, fines and arrests, and security checkpoints as part of imposed quarantine regimens. Given the time constraints and urgency of necessary action, such authoritarian measures will likely be cheered on by many people in the country.

My own view is that promoting an ethics of collective care and social solidarity is a better motivation for action and will yield better long-term results, because buy-in from citizens is based on altruism rather than threat or deterrence. For such a strategy of social solidarity to work it needs to be demonstrated, and some of this important work is already happening in mutual-aid networks springing up across the country, such as groups in Vancouver, Toronto, and Montreal that have been set up to find ways to share resources, to help those in need of deliveries or other kinds of care, to resist evictions, and to generally support the community in whatever ways possible.[6] It is only by showing social solidarity and actually demonstrating how it works that it can be built.

---

[6] A few of the earliest pandemic-related mutual-aid groups are still active as of early 2022. See, for example, the Facebook groups "COVID-19 Coming Together (Vancouver)," "How can I help COVID-19 Toronto," and "Montréal – Tio'tia:ke - Entraide - Mutual Aid."

So let us stop pointing fingers at the so-called bad and stupid people who do not follow the rules. Instead, let us look for ways to demonstrate the kind of collective care and social solidarity that we need.

The global battle for personal protective equipment turns ugly

Should personal protective equipment be distributed based on need or the market?

The competition for personal protective equipment has taken an ugly turn.[1] Amid a global shortage of PPE, countries have been competing for what is available in the global market, even as some states, including Canada, had previously been sharing and donating PPE to countries dealing with severe outbreaks.[2] Many countries are ramping up their production of medical masks, surgical gowns, face shields, and other gear required by healthcare workers treating COVID-19 patients.

Then last week, the United States invoked the Defense Production Act, which allows it to compel domestic companies to produce and distribute emergency goods in specific ways. Two incidents related to that country's moves to secure PPE have since figured in the public discussion north of the border. First, and most pressing for Canada, was President Trump's decision to order the company 3M to not ship N95 masks or other PPE to Canada. Several provincial-run healthcare organizations

---

[1] Published in *Ricochet*, April 7, 2020.

[2] In late January and early February 2020, for example, the federal government organized shipments of PPE to China.

have ongoing relationships with 3M, and they were relying on these shipments to shore up essential supplies for workers, which the Ontario provincial government has estimated could be depleted within a week. In a second incident, the German government accused the U.S. of "piracy" in taking a shipment of masks in Bangkok that was in transit from China to Germany. The German government said the U.S. was using "wild west" methods to secure PPE in the global market.

America first and Trump's pandering

The Canadian response to these American moves to secure PPE has ranged from anger to dismay to feelings of betrayal. While the Canadian federal government has maintained an even tone and encouraged constructive discussions with U.S. officials, as it has consistently done through numerous disputes over the last few years, provincial politicians opened fire.

Saskatchewan's premier Scott Moe called Trump's demand for 3M to not export PPE to Canada a betrayal. Ontario premier Doug Ford took aim at the U.S. president and vowed he would never again allow the province to be at the mercy of decisions made by the White House. And Newfoundland and Labrador's premier Dwight Ball said he was infuriated with the order and felt betrayed, even invoking his province's efforts to care for Americans stranded during 9/11.

Some of the colourful language used by Canadians on social media, compared to which the official political responses seem tame, shows that the public response was even more pointed. Trump's decision was viewed as a stab in the back, an affront to a history of close ties and integration of Canada and the United States. And of course the majority of the Canadian public also instinctively knew that Trump's order was as much about pandering to his base, another cynical ploy to curry favour and votes ahead of an election. This was as infuriating and hurtful for Canadians as the actual loss of PPE, since the well-being of Canadians became simply another rhetorical flourish for Trump to trot out during his daily self-congratulation speeches and adoration rallies.[3]

'Canada first'

It is difficult to separate what happens in the United States from the ongoing spectacle of Trump's presidency. At times it can also be difficult for Canadians to separate his odious antics and the crassness of U.S. politics generally from the American people themselves. However, I am asking, if only for the sake of thinking through the issue, that readers try for the moment to forget about Trump and try to put his narcissism in brackets. This is how we can move the discussion to ethics, and since Trump has none, he needs to be subtracted from the equation. The question, in a nutshell, is whether there is in fact a good reason that the United States deserves to have this PPE?

Now, to be clear, I think that Canadian healthcare workers should absolutely have the equipment necessary to work in a safe environment. They are afraid and anxious right now as they go to their jobs, and that is wrong. Everything that can be done for Canadian healthcare workers must be done. But I have not seen any evidence to suggest that Canada's need for PPE is greater than the need for PPE in the United States. It is actually quite the opposite: everything that I see in the media suggests that the United States is experiencing the pandemic in a far more

---

[3] There is probably an entire book to be written on only the impact that the Trump presidency had on Canada's pandemic response, and the smoldering bitterness between Trump and the Canadian political establishment across the spectrum. However, it is doubtful that even a more conventional U.S. president would not have done precisely the same things. Shortly after the Biden administration took over in the White House, they decided to continue the America-first policy on vaccinations and ruled out sending vaccines to Canada or Mexico.

acute way than Canada, and American healthcare workers are similarly experiencing shortages of PPE and facing unacceptable risks.

Can it be understood as justice and fairness that Americans get what might have been intended as Canadian PPE? If the United States is indeed facing a worse crisis and an even worse shortage of PPE, is it not incumbent on Canada to give up its claim to these resources in the name of the greater good?

I do not know if this can be quantified, but as so much of what is considered sound decision-making is based on numbers and empirical data, it would be interesting to know if there is a way to measure whose need is greater, Canada or the United States. In the absence of hard data, how else can we justify assertions that Canada should receive this PPE? Is it because we believe in a principle of free markets and unrestricted international movement of goods and services? And if so, how can that be squared with the increasing restrictions on the movement of goods and services that Canada has imposed during this crisis by closing its borders and protecting its own industries? And what does it say, furthermore, that Canada does not protest on behalf of the other countries specifically singled out by Trump's restrictions on 3M? Is the Canadian response of asking to be exempt from the U.S. emergency order any different from the U.S. response itself, in the sense that Canada is advocating only for itself and not calling for all countries to be exempt or for the order to be rescinded? Is it not simply a version of "Canada first"?

A global and international response

Obviously, we want what is best for our people and especially for our healthcare workers caring for patients with COVID-19. I do not think anyone will disagree that the shortage of PPE for Canadian workers is entirely unacceptable. But we should also recognize that the entire world is facing the exact same issue. And unfortunately, systems of global trade and international relations do not operate in the spirit of justice and fairness, even if laudable values are supposed to be the foundation of international politics and international institutions such as the United Nations and World Health Organization. The reality is quite the opposite. It is in many ways an international order in which might rules, a system that historically privileges wealthy and powerful countries ahead of others. As the pandemic is a truly global and international threat, it calls for a response that is likewise global and international, and it therefore calls for an ethics that takes into account more than national or provincial concerns.[4]

What is unfolding in this pandemic is undoubtedly a massive tragedy of human loss and suffering. It affects every country in the world, but not equally. Countries that were already the most vulnerable are more vulnerable still, and there are vulnerable communities and vulnerable groups within countries, even within rich countries, that are also made more vulnerable still. The issue of PPE is just one example of the ethical dilemmas the pandemic asks us to confront. Inasmuch as Canadians may say they will remember the way the U.S. president treated their country during a moment of need, people around the world will equally remember those nations who acted for the greater good.

---

[4] For an incisive analysis of the various ways that national borders and the so-called international order gets in the way of an effective response to global health emergencies, see Stephanie DeGooyer and Srinivas Murthy's "Health Nativism," *Dissent*, March 17, 2020.

The pandemic and social unrest

Even before the pandemic, we were living in a revolutionary age, and now long-standing injustices and inequalities are amplified by COVID-19

The pandemic is first of all a human tragedy, causing suffering and loss in an immediate and embodied way for millions of people all over the world.[1] But it is a crisis beyond just human health, in the sense that it disrupts and upends the economy, social relations, culture, and politics generally. One obvious outcome of the pandemic must be increased social unrest.

Here in the opening phases of the pandemic, there are lots of examples of people finding glimmers of hope and affirmations. In major cities people come out on their balconies and cheer for healthcare workers. There have been impromptu concerts and singing from rooftops to raise spirits. People are also rallying to their governments, as shown in recent Canadian polling data of a jump in support for federal and provincial leaders. Opinion polls even show that some 64% of Conservative voters in Canada support Justin Trudeau running whatever deficit is necessary

---

[1] Published in *The Independent NL*, April 23, 2020, as part of a COVID-19 series of articles called "Thinking outside the crisis," which was edited by Robin Whitaker.

to address the crisis, and an even greater number say they support the restrictions introduced so far.

Yet even as many are rallying to the flag and supporting their governments in these early days, the pandemic is fuelling social unrest and exposing injustice and inequality. As the crisis drags on, perhaps for many months or even years, the various levers the federal and provincial governments can pull to reduce the likelihood of unrest, like relief measures, may not remain viable. Following Lauren Berlant's analysis, the optimism that so many are keen to latch onto here in Canada may become cruel when the facade is torn away and when the grim reality of the situation becomes clear.[2] As happened in Italy, the singing will stop.[3]

Pandemic spurs ongoing unrest

It is worth remembering that in the year prior to the pandemic many countries were already experiencing significant unrest: the so-called Global Protest Wave of 2019. Moreover, the entire world has been in the throes of significant and recurrent waves of crisis, shock, and unrest since at least the 2008 financial crisis and the 2011-12 revolutionary wave that originated in the Arab Spring. Even before the pandemic arrived, we were living through a revolutionary age.

Now, against this background of ongoing protests, signs of social turmoil specifically related to the pandemic are starting to be reported in many countries, including Nigeria, El Salvador, Italy, Myanmar, China, Spain, Indonesia, Colombia, the United States, and the Philippines, to name a few. Although Canada has not seen a marked increase so far, the potential for

---

[2] Lauren Berlant, *Cruel Optimism*, Duke UP, 2011.

[3] Italy experienced an early outbreak, ahead of other Western countries. See Angela Giuffrida and Lorenzo Tondo, "Singing stops in Italy as fear and social unrest mount," *The Guardian*, April 1, 2020.

widespread social unrest is encouraged by growing numbers of people out of work and facing insecurity, and commentators have been quick to caution that the infringement on civil rights in the lockdown may itself be a source of unrest going forward. One particular concern for Canadians is also high levels of infections in the United States, plus the intensification of unrest in numerous U.S. states in response to lockdowns and restrictions. As the old saying goes, when America coughs Canada gets a cold.

As the pandemic unfolds

So that is something of the background and context of unrest globally and in Canada. What, then, may we expect to see?

To say that there will be increased social unrest resulting from the pandemic is not to speculate precisely where renewed and widespread social unrest may lead. There are other writers and theorists, including those contributing to this series in *The Independent NL*, who discuss the kinds of movements and political and social projects the pandemic makes possible or makes more likely, and no such projects can be carried out if they are not first imagined. In this light, the proliferation of calls from all sides for widespread and systemic change out of the pandemic is both noteworthy and welcome.

Most descriptions of the kinds of possible futures that may emerge out of the present crisis, whether utopian, authoritarian, or otherwise, presuppose unrest but seldom mention it. We seem to intuitively understand, as Arundhati Roy points out in a recent article, that the pandemic is a portal, and perhaps this is an important initial takeaway.[4] It will be in the context of unrest or because of unrest that any political projects become possible.

It is also crucially important to recognize the enormous disparities of the impacts of the pandemic on different countries

---

[4] Arundhati Roy, "The pandemic is a portal," *FT*, April 3, 2020.

and regions, and between different communities within any given country. As I said above, long-standing and unaddressed injustices and inequalities are magnified by the pandemic. It is these systemic failings, or these all-too-perfect operations of systems doing what they were designed to do, that are the fuel of unrest, as the pandemic may be the spark.

Poorer countries will be most vulnerable to mass dissidence and uprisings resulting from the pandemic, partly because many poorer countries are already dealing with various kinds of instability. For many of the world's poorest people, self-isolating and physical distancing is simply not possible, water is scarce, and there is little or no access to health care. Even in developing countries like Brazil and India, where standards of living have risen in recent decades, huge numbers of people live in slums and favelas, and it is these areas that will predictably be where the pandemic has the worst effects and also where unrest will grow.

But because the pandemic is by definition global, its impacts will be confined to no one country, rich or poor. This has led to calls from economists to recognize that any economic and social implosions in poor and developing countries will have serious knock-on effects in rich countries. Everyone is in this together, even if the suffering and hardships are not equitably distributed. This realization, cynically viewed, has provided the impetus for an unprecedented International Monetary Fund program of debt cancellation for some of the poorest countries in the world.[5] Such measures aim to shore up poor and developing countries as a bulwark for the rich, since the cascade effects of collapsing or failed economies in the current context may be a threat to

---

[5] See International Monetary Fund report, "COVID-19 Financial Assistance and Debt Service Relief," March 2020. Debt cancellations and renegotiations for poor countries continued throughout the pandemic.

the entire global financial system. Of course, one can expect that if the emergency situation somehow comes to a swift resolution, this supposed act of compassion and benevolence will quickly be rescinded.

Power responds

So then, how will states respond to unrest? Increasing unrest will mean a direct challenge to power in many countries, and authoritarian and despotic regimes will respond in the only ways they know how: with direct violence. It should not come as a surprise to see some governments fall, but neither should it be surprising to see some governments retain power through brutality. A recent example of such brutality is in the severe crackdown in Nigeria, where security forces have killed more people than the virus.[6]

An entirely different and somewhat surreal example of power responding is unfolding in the U.S., where the president seems to be actively encouraging unrest. Of course, many of the rallies in recent days have been carried out by the president's base of supporters, some of whom are tied in with militia movements and other elements on the far-right of American politics. This points to another possible form of response, since opportunistic strongman politicians may view the crisis as a way to secure more power. Those in power will sometimes invite and promote unrest in the service of their own political projects.[7] Again, I am

---

[6] In March 2020, reports emerged of Nigerian security services shooting people who broke lockdown. At that time, at least according to official accounts, only two people had died in the country because of the virus, but dozens were killed by police crackdowns. There are reports from several other countries of the same kind of authoritarian responses. See the Amnesty International report, "COVID-19 crackdowns: Police abuse and the global pandemic," December 2020.

[7] Reflecting on this after the fact, the ways that Trump purposefully stoked unrest gave some indication of the eventual January 6, 2021,

not making predictions about what may happen in any given country, but the pandemic and the unrest it generates will make coups much more possible.

Finally, as has been the case in some countries already, an expanded surveillance apparatus is another possible response. For example, a phone app is being used in South Korea that alerts people when they are near a confirmed COVID-19 case. Meanwhile, Australia is preparing an app that allows for contact tracing by tracking everywhere an infected person has been for the previous weeks. China uses an app that colour-codes people and says who may or may not leave their house, and Poland has an app that obliges people to photograph themselves to prove they are home. Polling data in Canada suggests the public in this country strongly approve of expanding surveillance in the context of the pandemic.[8] It is a simple step for such expanded surveillance to be bootstrapped into quelling unrest.

The right to revolution

On the one hand it seems easy to say that during a global health emergency, revolution should be put on hold. However, the conditions of life in many places dictate that the pandemic will simply increase the likelihood of unrest, uprising, and revolt. This may very well have consequences for the number who may eventually die from the pandemic, but such revolutions cannot be expected to wait. Nothing was being done to address the conditions that made unrest possible before the pandemic. So

---

attack on the capitol in Washington, D.C., even at this early stage of the pandemic.

[8] Months later the government released the COVID alert app to the public. The app had some initial uptake, but not enough people ended up downloading or using the app to make it helpful. According to an April 2021 York University study, it was downloaded 6.4 million times and only 25,000 people input information of a positive test.

now, when desperate people are even more desperate still, those existing injustices and inequalities will not be contained.

Unfortunately, it is also a time of crisis in which many people are singularly worried about their own families or communities. In this sense the pandemic may provide a kind of cover or fog, as each nation looks inward, that enables authoritarianism and brutality. And it is for this reason that we must be alert to what happens in other places and show solidarity with the struggles of oppressed people everywhere.

With respect to our own country, everything is by no means perfect here in Canada. It is true that we have a public healthcare system and some forms of social security. And it is unlikely we will see the extent of unrest that may sweep through poor and developing countries hand in hand with the pandemic. However, we should look to the numerous unaddressed injustices in this country as catalysts for a marked increase in unrest in Canada in the coming months and years. Buckle up.

A wave of mass social unrest lies on the horizon

*Pandemic protesters may seem ridiculous
but worsening conditions will lead to
justified resistance and unrest*

The protests springing up across the United States in response to pandemic lockdowns and restrictions are an easy target for ridicule.[1] People claiming restrictions should be lifted because they need to get a haircut while thousands die every day is a display of callousness and stupidity beyond the pale, even by American standards. But attributing the protests to pure and simple stupidity fails to account for burgeoning and justifiable social unrest resulting from the pandemic in the U.S., Canada, and all over the world.

To be clear, most of the images we are seeing of the protests coming out of the U.S. are of militia members, MAGA hats, and fundamentalist Christians, all the worst elements of far-right American politics. For many of these people, the main purpose of going to anti-lockdown protests seems to be to "own the libs," which seemingly takes precedence over the basic biological drive of self-preservation. It is difficult to overstate the cynicism of

---

[1] Published in *Ricochet*, April 27, 2020.

pandemic protesters holding signs with the slogan "my body, my choice."[2] None of this is worthy of support and is rightly being called out. Let us be clear about that.

Some reasons beyond stupidity

But these are not the views of everyone taking part in the protests. The images and flashpoints of far-right stupidity are simply the focal point for an American mainstream media that is, by and large, hopelessly mired in partisanship. In American political discourse, what might be called the "left" has a singular focus to "own the Republicans" and "own Trump." Basically nothing of what we see emanating from mainstream U.S. media attempts to explain anything.

Some people are taking part in the protests out of much more genuine and understandable concerns, as Ben Burgis discusses in an article in Jacobin.[3] Recent figures suggest that some 26 million Americans are unemployed, or roughly one in six working-age people in the country. The pandemic is causing a calamity of unemployment to rival the Great Depression. And this in a country with staggering inequality, basically no social security net, and a federal government with little financial room to maneuver in providing relief. Is uncertainty about providing for one's family not a perfectly justifiable reason for protest?

In a similar light, compare your gut reaction to the news of pandemic protests in the U.S. with news of similar protests in other countries, including recent demonstrations in Germany,

---

[2] This slogan came from the pro-choice movement and is a good indication of the cynicism of the anti-lockdown protests, since many of the right-wing fringe and evangelicals in the Trump camp are part of the so-called pro-life movement. To have them use this slogan is a good example of their underlying motivation to lash out at liberals.

[3] Ben Burgis, "The left can't just dismiss the anti-lockdown protests," *Jacobin*, April 23, 2020.

Poland, Nigeria, El Salvador, Italy, Russia, Myanmar, China, Spain, Indonesia, Colombia, the Philippines, France, Lebanon, and several other countries. Lebanon, for instance, had massive protests throughout 2019 related to unemployment, corruption, and ongoing economic crisis. Protesters demanded an end to a government based on power-sharing among civil war–era factions. The pandemic and the lockdown in the country have further magnified these concerns. And remember also that the pandemic struck in the wake of, or in addition to, an enormous global wave of protests in 2019, the grievances of which have by and large not been resolved. Looking at pandemic protests in Lebanon and in other countries, it is possible to decry them as unsafe and unhelpful while a health crisis is unfolding. But it is also easy to understand why they are happening and why they are in many ways justified.

A new era of unrest

Simply put, the pandemic is intensifying ongoing injustice and inequality all over the world. As a stark example, recent reports predict the pandemic will double the number of people facing starvation across the globe.[4] Here in Canada, the impacts of the pandemic may not be so extreme, but surging unemployment will push many more into poverty and homelessness. Many communities already reeling from injustice and inequality will see conditions get worse.

There have only been a few very small protests in Canada specifically related to the lockdown and the pandemic so far, and these are perhaps closer to the protests in the U.S. than they are to protests in countries like Lebanon that are directly

---

[4] See the study "2020 global report on food crises," Food Security Information Network, April 20, 2020; and Marc F. Bellemare, "Rising food prices, food price volatility, and social unrest," *American Journal of Agricultural Economics* 97.1, 2015.

connected with recent uprisings. But the point here is that as the pandemic unfolds over the coming months and possibly years, and as its effects are felt by everyday people for much longer than that, there will be growing unrest. And this unrest, with predictable protests and acts of resistance, is entirely justified.

So by all means, let us call out the dangerous elements of the far-right in American protests, and let us ridicule any similar tendencies here in Canada or other parts of the world. But let us also expand the analysis beyond just pointing at stupidity to see the wave of mass social unrest on the horizon.

Forcing workers back could reignite class warfare

Bosses should not be surprised by worker resistance during a pandemic that threatens their well-being

Renewed class consciousness among workers may quickly show those pushing to hastily reopen workplaces that they have bitten off more than they can chew.[1] From "stay home at all costs" to "get back to work," the pandemic narrative and key messaging coming from government and business leaders has dramatically shifted in recent weeks.

Some voices, especially from more conservative corners, have questioned the work ethic of the underclass, even suggesting that low-income workers are lazy and will need to be coerced into returning to their jobs, as Ethan Cox notes in a recent article for *Ricochet*.[2] The kinds of workers most often under attack are those in precarious situations, minimum-wage workers, migrant workers, and workers in low-wage industries. This includes workers in manufacturing and production, like at the Cargill slaughterhouse, which has been front and centre in news

---

[1] Published in *Ricochet*, May 12, 2020.

[2] Ethan Cox, "Trading our lives for their profits: The plan to sacrifice low-wage workers," *Ricochet*, May 7, 2020.

reports as the site of the largest COVID-19 outbreak in North America. It also includes service industry workers, retail and sales staff, cleaners, childcare providers, gym attendants, and others in workplaces that function through high levels of contact with the public.[3] These workers are for the most part non-unionized and have essentially no job security and no ability to raise concerns with employers, even as they are facing high levels of risk.

Employment lawyers are keen to point out that workers have no right to refuse to go back to work if they are recalled from layoffs, even in the midst of a pandemic. If they do refuse, or so the lawyers say, they will be considered to have quit their jobs and therefore become ineligible for employment insurance or the Canadian Emergency Response Benefit (CERB).[4] Workers must, so the narrative goes, be threatened and then punished if there is any resistance to the demands of employers. By threatening to make a worker ineligible for EI or the CERB,

---

[3] The outbreak at the Cargill meat-packing plant resulted in the deaths of several employees and raised the issue of worker protections in the early stages of the pandemic in Canada. Many workplaces installed plastic dividers and instituted other forms of hygiene theatre in order to manage perceptions. See Andrew Jeffrey, "Stress and fear in the factories: The toll taken by COVID-19 inside some busy Alberta workplaces," *CBC*, April 9, 2021.

[4] In early May 2020, there was a flurry of stories highlighting that workers could not refuse to return to their jobs. Looking back now, with the pandemic entering its third year, it appears even more cold-hearted that such stories were promoted, likely by PR groups working on behalf of business interests. At the same time, business groups were also promoting the idea that mental health was one of the main reasons that the economy needed to be swiftly reopened, such as an open letter to Newfoundland and Labrador premier Dwight Ball that breathlessly called for business to be reopened out of compassion for the well-being of children. See Alexandra Mae Jones, "Do you have the right to refuse to return to work?" *CTV*, May 7, 2020; Ania Bessonov and Amil Niazi, "Do I have the right to refuse work?" *CBC*, May 11, 2020; and "Reopen economy fully, and soon, business leaders tell Ball in hard-hitting letter," *CBCNL*, June 12, 2020.

an employer is threatening that worker with destitution. And in this way, the same mechanisms brought forward by government to encourage and enable workers to participate in a project of collective care, the social project of "flattening the curve," have become a cattle prod to force them back into workplaces where they feel unsafe.

But then what?

There is a major error in the thinking on the part of those who are howling to reopen the economy and coerce workers back into jobs that put them at risk. In their zeal to prove who is in charge and to put profit ahead of the health and well-being of workers, they neglect to consider what may happen after such a display of arrogance.[5]

The contemporary workplace and management principles are grounded in notions of corporate social responsibility and social purpose. At some point in the last few decades, it became not only unpopular but impractical for any company to openly admit that their only reason for existing was to make money. Forcing workers back into jobs during a pandemic destroys that veneer, proving to employees and to the public the company is inauthentic. Leaving aside just this reputational damage, coercing workers back into jobs, and using government mechanisms to make that happen, also rips away the veil to show that workers today are no different from their counterparts generations ago. It shows workers that they are not free agents or freelancers "gigging" their way to prosperity, but are still fundamentally serfs bound to wage labour, like the coerced workers of earlier industrial phases of development.

---

[5] Here in 2022, I have to wonder what role some of these displays of arrogance by employers played in generating the initial energy for the anti-work movement and the so-called Great Resignation that are now in full swing.

In effect, this coercion vividly demonstrates to workers that they are part of a particular class, while the owners are part of a different class, and that the interests of these classes are not at all the same. Forcing workers back pops the bright balloons of corporate social responsibility and the narrative of workers as engaged stakeholders in companies, and instead reinstates class antagonisms that these balloons were supposed to mask.

The new normal is the old normal

Following this line of thought, in the newly reopened economy there may be a significant number of unhappy workers being coerced back to jobs, and some of these unhappy workers will return to these jobs with an emergent class consciousness. How will they act in the workplace?

Likely they will act much the same as their counterparts acted two generations ago. They have learned a bit about employment law and about the mechanisms of government being used against them, and some of them will start looking for similar mechanisms to use against employers, such as filing reports or calling for inspections over health and safety concerns. Some of them will find ways to use the system against those employers who treat them poorly or coerce them. It is only natural.

They will be more apt to absenteeism and calling in sick, and will use any and all legal means at their disposal to bend the rules in their favour. They will also not be enthusiastic in their work or in their roles as representatives of the company in their dealings with customers or clients. But not all workers will be in a position to enact resistance openly, and so some may resort to more subtle methods of sabotage. Any workplace is suscepti-ble to sabotage, since workers simply need to find a weakness or choke point in the workflow and production. Coerced, unhappy, or threatened workers will also be much more likely to see the clear benefits of organization and collective power in unions.

All these strategies and tactics of quagmire, sabotage, and organization are old and proven. And while there is no guarantee of their success in achieving workers' aims or in any broader struggle, workers can execute them in a decentralized manner, without needing any direction, and they will cause a major issue for any employer who is targeted.

Maybe we should thank them

Obviously, it is morally bankrupt for employers to try to coerce workers back into jobs during a pandemic. My hunch is that it is as much a power play as a necessity, in the sense that some of the people in authority are eager to assert their dominance and re-establish the hierarchy and social order that has been disrupted by the crisis. But nefarious as it is, perhaps we should thank the owners and bosses for dutifully playing their roles. They couldn't help themselves, so intrinsically are they tied to their dogma and ideology, and have done so without seriously considering the unintended consequences their actions may bring with respect to labour unrest.

It is true as well that not every business will act in this coercive and callous manner. It is an opportunity for any company with authentic foundations in corporate social responsibility and social purpose, and any company seriously committed to the well-being of workers, to show its true colours.

Either way, the narrative has shifted and the new normal of class antagonism is being thrust upon many workers. And let us be clear that workers did not create this antagonism or bring it to light in this instance. Employers and their ideological puppets did that all on their own. As usual, they will be shocked and aghast at the creative ways workers resist, to the point they may well wish they never went down this road in the first place.

What explains the Canadian failure on COVID-19?

Similar measures implemented in other countries were more successful

Try to talk about the abysmal performance of Canadians during the pandemic and you can expect to be met with a chorus of whataboutism and deflection.[1] Point to developing countries with comparatively scant resources like Vietnam, a country of 95 million with 1,537 COVID cases and 35 deaths, and some will say they hid the true figures. Point to developed countries like Japan, with 126 million people and 4,300 COVID deaths, and some will say they have a weaker strain of the virus, or will attribute Japan's success to the country's high levels of existing vaccination for tuberculosis.

It makes little difference the examples one may point to, there will always be some excuse for why what is happening in Canada, a country of 37 million people with over 18,000 COVID deaths, or roughly one in every 2,100 people, isn't as bad as it looks. What about this? What about that? What about this other thing? And after all, at least our situation is better than in our traditional punching bag, the United States of America.

---

[1] Published in *Ricochet*, January 18, 2021.

Whataboutism and deflection are easy ways to assuage guilt and avoid having to ask difficult questions.[2] But with case counts skyrocketing and the death count mounting, at some point these strategies of denial will stop working. People in this country are going to start asking how things have gone so terribly wrong.

The blame game

It was the government's fault, some will say. They waffled on the masks and the official communications plan was unclear. Or the government did not do enough to protect older adults in care homes. Or the government did not implement lockdowns at the right time. Or any number of other similar complaints about the government.

Certainly it is true that all levels of government across Canada have responsibilities for decisions that were taken and the ways they communicated with the public. But entirely blaming the government is another deflection, a way of avoiding personal and collective responsibility. And again, governments in many countries with significantly less resources enacted essentially the same restrictions and policies, and the results have often been far better than in Canada.

Well then, it was the bad apples, some will say. What can you do? There are always going to be these kinds of people who are irresponsible and just will not follow the rules. There is simply no reasoning with some people.

It is of course perfectly true that there are individuals who have all along stubbornly refused to take even the most basic of

---

[2] Along with there being an element of denial in this, there is also some element of what Lauren Berlant calls "cruel optimism," which is a devotion to an affirmative perspective on a situation that creates an inability to confront a harsh reality or do anything about it. In this case, the desire to be optimistic about one's country and community contributes to an inability to perceive or do anything about an ethical failure. See Lauren Berlant, *Cruel Optimism*, Duke UP, 2011.

precautions for their own safety or the safety of others. However, presumably the argument must be, then, that comparatively speaking Canada has more ignorant or irresponsible people than other countries, and that somehow the actions of individuals do not ultimately add up to a collective condemnation.

The uncomfortable truth

Part of the uncomfortable truth Canadians are starting to come around to is that we have collectively failed.[3] Canadians failed to come together in the face of adversity, failed to protect some of the most vulnerable people in society, and failed this test of social solidarity and common decency.[4] It is only a matter of looking at what is happening right now in our own cities and towns, recognizing the victims, and understanding that all this suffering did not have to happen. Recognizing failure, the main question becomes, how did everything go so terribly wrong? Is there something about the character of this country and its people, some underlying social, cultural, or economic factors that contributed to this failure? Because at the end of the day, the obvious difference between Canada and other countries with respect to the pandemic is, quite simply, that Canada is populated by Canadians.

So even though it is true that different people and different communities may have more or less direct responsibility for this failure, it is in the first instance a collective failure and needs to be recognized as such. It is a failure, writ large, of basic human decency. The effects of failure go beyond the terrible

---

[3] Thinking about this further, I am not sure that Canadians are coming around to this realization. The opposite is probably true, and people are doing whatever they can to avoid having to confront what happened in this country during the pandemic.

[4] As the reader will be able to tell, this was the point where my views on what was happening in Canada as it relates to ethics and the COVID-19 pandemic shifted.

cost in human life and suffering, to also destroy relationships, shatter communities, and undermine the fundamental idea of what it is to be Canadian. It will have a profound impact on every aspect of our country in the years to come.[5]

---

[5] By early February 2022, about a year after the materials for this chapter were written, it was becoming increasingly clear that social cohesion in Canada was fraying. One example was the anti-mandate and anti-vaccine protests, which had spiralled into something like a large-scale populist uprising and occupation of Ottawa. Later in this book, I focus on some of the impacts of various pandemic-related failures, specifically in the chapters "The pandemic and social relations," and "COVID-19 and the unravelling of Canadian identity."

The failure of common decency

There will be a great impulse to cover over and deny such a failure ever happened

Since the beginning of the COVID-19 outbreak in Canada, I have tried to understand the pandemic in relation to ethics.[1] The question, in a nutshell, is what does it mean to act ethically in the face of the COVID-19 outbreak in Canada? I do not believe there is one straightforward answer, but I propose, for the sake of the discussion to follow, that simply put, ethical action in a pandemic is common decency.

I offer this simple axiom in order to create a vantage point from which a further question can be explored: what is the degree to which Canadians have enacted common decency in the face of the pandemic?

A novel framework

An exploration of this type needs some kind of rubric or model, a way to assess what happened in order to draw conclusions. For such a model I look to Albert Camus' philosophical novel *The Plague*. In this book, Camus explores this very question, and even in the face of an outbreak of disease, as the main

---

[1] Published in *Ricochet*, February 3, 2021.

theme of the novel. More generally, it can be understood as a thought experiment into the question of what simple human decency looks like.[2]

In *The Plague*, Camus goes to great lengths to make clear that he is not so much interested in extravagant or magnanimous efforts. He is not talking about the heroic at all. He points out that there is something perverse about focusing on supposedly heroic figures in times of calamity like plagues or pandemics. For Camus, the most important acts are the simple and common acts of everyday people: "There's no question of heroism in all this. It's a matter of common decency. That's an idea which may make some people smile, but the only means of fighting a plague is common decency."

Common decency, as Camus understands it, requires that people accept the unfairness and absurdity of the situation in which they find themselves, and then choose to act in a way that takes into account the needs of those around them and of the community of which they are a part. Again, this notion is not about valiant heroism or grand acts. It involves simple things like empathy, understanding, and patience. It is simply doing what is required of decent human beings by the situation, no more and no less.

In the closing pages of the book, Camus offers something of an evaluation based on his novelistic engagement with the question of common decency: "To state quite simply what we

---

[2] For anyone who has not read *The Plague*, it is striking just how many of the things that happen in Camus' fictional community also happened throughout the pandemic. In the introduction of this book, I noted three categories of subjectivity that emerge as responses to the pandemic: ethical subjectivity, passive nihilism, and active nihilism. Those three categories are also evident in Camus' novel, and I feel have some representative or comparative value in the breakdown of "decency," "in-between," and "indecency" as I discuss in this chapter, although I do not make that explicit in the discussion to follow.

learn in a time of pestilence: that there are more things to admire in people than to despise." Of course, throughout the book there are many examples of failures of common decency, but when weighing separately the good and the bad and taking all things into account, on the whole Camus finds that common decency wins out.

Weighing decency

Now to our own situation and the question of common decency during the pandemic in Canada. Let us imagine a set of scales, and on one side of the balance are the decent acts, while on the other are the indecent acts. Which way will the scales tip?

One thing to remember about acts of common decency is that they are very often unseen and unrecorded, whereas indecent acts are often all too visible and publicized, so care must be taken to give wide latitude for measuring what is decent. For example, decent acts like helping out a neighbour with a load of groceries or keeping up a regular phone call with someone who has no family are extremely common and happen all the time.

And overall, many millions of people in this country have done what is necessary to adjust to a new normal by altering their routines, working from home, taking on responsibility for educating young people, and generally all the sacrifices people made and are continuing to make during the various lockdowns. This has been a trying time, and many people all across Canada have done their part in simple, often overlooked ways, even at the cost of personal hardship. That so many people are willing to make these sacrifices for the well-being of others is certainly a general vote in favour of the decency of people in Canada.

Without needing to call it heroism, all the people that are called frontline workers also contribute to the overall measure of common decency. This is people doing what they need to do and what they are called upon to do in their specific occupation or community role. Indeed, even those people who have found themselves unemployed have a role to play, in the sense that what they are called upon to do is to just stay home and interact with as few people as possible. Never has decency been so easy (or so difficult, as shall be seen below).

Weighing the in-between

Since common decency is not exactly something that can be measured with a ruler or under an electron microscope, there is no way to scientifically quantify it. For this reason, it is necessary to give a wide range for what common decency might mean, as above in the exceedingly simple gestures that weigh in its favour.

But note that decency is not by definition about following a set of prescribed rules, such as the restrictions (or lack thereof) set out by governments throughout Canada. For example, just because the government said it was okay for people to travel around the country in the summer months does not mean that doing so was an act of common decency. No one is called upon to go on a road trip in the name of the common good.

Similarly, look at going out to restaurants, shopping, hosting events, and other such activities. Governments came out with regulations for all manner of things and said that it was okay to act in particular ways. But all those actions and the rules that enabled them need to be laid against the backdrop of what has actually happened with the pandemic. All those actions created the conditions, biologically, socially, and culturally, for a great deal of unnecessary suffering. There is no decency in this, but nor is it necessarily fair (since the bar is set so low) to call such actions indecent.

Still, it seems necessary to account for this in-between, as it allows us to better understand what is actually going on the scales. Again, highlighting the in-between is useful to give a wide berth for decency and indecency. It is not that going on road trips or going shopping or celebrating holidays is indecent, but those actions, nonetheless, are also not expressions of solidarity, and are potentially thoughtless of the needs of others or lacking in fulsome empathy.

Weighing indecency

Categorizing a particular action or attitude as indecent is something there will inevitably be lots of disagreement about. As I mentioned at the opening of this article, the main purpose of positing the axiom that ethical action in a pandemic is common decency is to create a vantage point from which a discussion may take place. Each of us will ultimately have to decide for ourselves what counts as decent or indecent. Here are a few that have occurred to me and that I have observed over the last weeks and months.

It is indecent that so many older adults in care homes have died. These older adults are often in vulnerable situations, isolated from their families and the people who care for them, and often have other health conditions that may contribute to the precariousness of their situation. It is a national outrage that many thousands of older adults have died in care homes, and even more outrageous that the underlying reasons are often to do with an ongoing lack of funding, poor pay for healthcare workers, and what amounts to a general social acceptance of the disposability of older people.

It is indecent that many racialized communities have borne a disproportionate share of death and suffering in the pandemic in Canada. In my own city of Toronto, it has been the areas in the North York district such as the racialized and underserved

Jane-Finch neighbourhood that have been hit particularly hard, while relatively affluent and predominantly white areas in the Old Toronto neighbourhoods have been mostly spared. Some of the reasons for this are because people in poor or racialized neighbourhoods do not have the same opportunities or the same privilege to choose to self-isolate or work from home.[3]

It is indecent that people experiencing homelessness have not received the support or care they need to stay healthy and survive during the pandemic in Canada. In recent weeks there have been reports of overwhelmed shelters in Canadian cities, such as was recently reported in *Ricochet* about shelters in Montreal.[4] Programs to support people experiencing homelessness that were in place through the warmer months of the summer and fall, when they were less needed, have now been discontinued. And here in the coldest months when people need to be indoors, an outbreak at a shelter or care facility means that no one can stay there.

Looking outside our own borders, it is indecent that any kind of public discussion took place about whether this country was at the front of the line for global access to vaccines. Currently, the Canadian government has ordered or pre-ordered more than seven vaccine doses per Canadian, while there is no clear short- or medium-term plan for vaccinations for most of the African continent. A recent report by Amnesty International suggests that Canada is among the worst vaccine hoarders on the planet.[5] In recent days the World Health Organization has

---

[3] This inequity was further brought to light during the initial phases of the vaccine rollout, when affluent neighborhoods of the city, which had the lowest levels of infection, were the first to be vaccinated.

[4] Christopher Curtis, "'Worst-case scenario': COVID-19 outbreak hits Montreal homeless shelters," *Ricochet*, January 4, 2021.

[5] Tamaryn Nelson, "Rich Western countries are hoarding COVID-19 vaccines," Amnesty International, January 5, 2021.

said vaccine hoarding is driving up prices, limiting access for poor countries, and constitutes a catastrophic moral failure.[6]

It is indecent that business and financial interests cynically expressed concern for the mental health of Canadians as a ploy to remove restrictions on their activities. It is indecent that so many frontline workers are subjected to unnecessary risks in the name of the economy. It is indecent that a significant portion of the population refuses to simply wear a mask. And on and on...

It is indecent that the vast collective called "the Canadian people" stands by and does nothing as the most vulnerable among them, and the most vulnerable around the world, bear the brunt of the pandemic, suffer, and die.

How the scales tip

It may sound harsh, but with respect to the Canadian response to COVID-19, I find it difficult to think of any greater ethical wrong that has been so obviously committed in such a short period of time in living memory in this country. Certainly there have been individual and collective acts of decency that are worthy of admiration. But following the rubric of Camus' thought experiment, I cannot imagine any clear argument in favour of the overall decency in any of this (or I would love to hear it, anyways). If ethical action in a pandemic is common decency, then we have failed.

What this failure points to is a lack of values, or, rather, to a misplaced set of values. It is simply a matter of looking at where things have broken down and asking what would have needed to happen for it to be different. And in the most egregious cases of indecency, it is clear that the dominant ideological forces at

---

[6] Tedros Adhanom Ghebreyesus, "Opening remarks at 148th session of the Executive Board," January 18, 2021.

work in our society value profit over lives. It would simply have taken a little bit of money. If the pandemic is a looking-glass, it shows us a Canadian society in which economics is more important than morality. Or said another way, a society in which right and wrong is determined by economics instead of ethical principles.

Beyond the unnecessary death and suffering visited upon people who were made disposable, the broader impacts of this ethical failure are only now coming into view. For example, many Canadians like to think of themselves as living in caring communities with strong bonds of social solidarity. Outside our own borders, many Canadians like to see themselves as a moral and ethical compass for humanitarianism in the world.

What happens to a society when its foundational narratives and markers of collective identity are so clearly unravelled? What does it do to relationships and basic social bonds when people perceive their own family, friends, and communities as complicit in such indecency? These are some of the questions that Canadians are now called upon to answer. Of course, many people will want to forget about all this as quickly as possible, and there will be a great impulse to cover over and deny such a failure of common decency ever happened. And because past behaviour is the best predictor of future behaviour, it is questionable if Canadian society has the fortitude to truly take stock of something so obscene.

The ethics of antibodies

If the idea is for everyone to develop antibodies against COVID-19, the way that happens matters

Antibodies are part of the mechanism the immune system uses to fight off threats like viruses.[1] COVID-19 vaccines prompt the production of protective antibodies, just as COVID-19 infection elicits protective antibodies. The idea underlying vaccines is that it is better to get antibodies through vaccination rather than through the full brunt of a natural infection. That's why, if you are able, you should get vaccinated. Let's be clear about that. This discussion of the ethics of antibodies is not an anti-vaccine message. If you are able to get vaccinated, you should.

The emerging trend in several countries, and what is taking shape in Canada, is to allow everyone to produce antibodies in search of elusive so-called herd immunity.[2] However, the way

---

[1] This chapter, written in mid-August 2021, was not previously published.

[2] Researchers and epidemiologists have mostly discredited the idea that COVID-19 can be brought under control by herd immunity, and the concept has somewhat fallen out of vogue. See Christie Aschwanden, "Five reasons why COVID herd immunity is probably impossible," *Nature*, March 18, 2021; and also Gypsyamber D'Souza and David Dowdy, "Rethinking herd immunity and the COVID-19 response end game," Bloomberg School of Public Health, September 13, 2021.

that some of these countries are looking to go about this is through unchecked infection. These are wealthy countries with significant vaccine coverage like Canada, the U.K., and the U.S. Yet still not enough people have antibodies to prevent widespread community transmission of the virus. The unspoken strategy is to allow the natural production of antibodies in those not vaccinated, up to whatever point is necessary in order to keep the virus at bay.

Part of the reason wealthy countries appear to be letting COVID-19 off the leash is pandemic fatigue. In some circles, the sentiment is "enough is enough" since the virus refuses to conform to the social, political, and economic rules. However, significant parts of the population are unvaccinated. And unvaccinated people are not a homogenous group. It includes people under the age of 12 and people who have compromised immune systems. It also includes people with perfectly valid reasons to distrust the government or the healthcare system. Some people are excluded or "illegal" and they cannot access vaccines. Some vaccine-hesitant people are legitimately frightened.

Nonetheless, a consensus is forming that a large percentage of the population will be sacrificed to be ravaged by the virus. Then everyone develops antibodies, society reaches some level of immunity to supposedly keep the virus at bay, and, according to the belief, "normality" resumes.

What is sad about this approach is that it is, once again, going to put some of the most vulnerable people at risk. By letting the virus off the leash and allowing unchecked infection, people who are at greatest risk, like people with disabilities and older adults, are being given no choice and are being excluded from society. This is why it has always been wrong and mean-spirited to just accept that the virus is going to be here to stay, instead of making every possible effort to eradicate it, as some regions of the world and even some regions of our country did for a time. It also shows that even if the virus is here to stay, it is wrong to allow it to spread unchecked in the population, without any efforts at control. Those types of choices are, by extension, decisions that amount to purposeful endangerment and exclusion of many of our fellow citizens. Some people just cannot safely develop antibodies, and so they will need to isolate for good to avoid the virus or risk dying.

It is a real dilemma, because there is, on the one hand, such enormous pressure to have life go back to something like it was before the pandemic began. But the trade-off for that, as it is now taking shape, is that people will need to be sacrificed. How many is Canada willing to sacrifice, and how much needs to be gained to make such sacrifices acceptable? And once a society begins down that path of finding it acceptable to sacrifice a particular kind of people and some percentage of the population, what else will it learn to justify, and where does it end?

Anti-vaccine protests and blame-shifting COVID-19 ethical responsibility in Canada

An unwillingness to engage with any valid reasons for anti-vaccine sentiment encourages scapegoating

When I saw images of anti-vaccine protesters demonstrating in front of hospitals, I was enraged.[1] It is callous and selfish to protest against the healthcare workers who have cared for our communities throughout the pandemic. Seeing images of anti-vaccine protesters wearing the Star of David in reference to their supposed persecution was even more shocking again. These incidents were so jarring that I had to stop and ask, what is going through their heads that they think this is appropriate?

As someone who researches protest movements, I know that dissent is often understood in radically different ways by the general public than by protesters themselves. That difference can be so great that those inside a dissident worldview and those outside see the same thing in completely opposite ways.

Take for example the case of the Branch Davidians and the Waco siege. The Davidians believed in an apocalyptic creed,

---

[1] This chapter is an expanded version of a research brief that was written in early September 2021.

and so when federal agents showed up at their compound, they did not perceive it as a government raid to seize illegal firearms but as signalling the first stage of the end of days, as David Koresh had prophesied. Much of the scholarship about the Waco siege argues that the inability of either side to comprehend the opposing worldview caused so many unnecessary deaths.

To be clear, I am not saying the anti-vaccine protesters are the same as the Davidians. I am also not saying that I sympathize with their cause. What I am saying is that the worldview of the anti-vaccine protests is radically different than the status quo, and an inability to understand that sentiment on its own terms gets in the way of doing anything about it.

Creating the scapegoat

Readers who would like to learn more of the long and complex history of the anti-vaccine movement should skip ahead to the next chapter of this book. It is an important context, and it is important to take anti-vaccine perspectives seriously, if only to be better able to dismantle those arguments. What I want to do here in this chapter is not so much try to understand anti-vaxxers, but rather to understand the failure on the part of the mainstream to authentically engage their worldview, especially since so much research exists on the subject.

For example, media representations of anti-vaccine protests generally make no attempt to understand or highlight legitimate concerns in the movement. Most news outlets pride themselves on some notion of journalistic objectivity, but the clear tone of mockery and derision in most articles about the anti-vaccine protests is obvious. It is a similar sort of caricaturing that can happen with almost any protest movement.

I am sure that many share my own shocked reaction and my immediate gut feeling of outrage at seeing the hospital protests. I have heard a wide range of rhetoric about how anti-vaxxers should be treated, including the openly expressed sentiment that they should be denied healthcare and left to die. Not only is there no attempt to understand the anti-vaccine movement, but the vitriol directed toward the anti-vaxxers is glaring when viewed dispassionately.

In fact, what it begins to look like is classic scapegoating. The definition of scapegoating is when the guilt of a community is placed upon some object or individuals, which is then cast out to absolve sins. Scapegoating is often described as an irrational act because the object, group, or individual that takes the blame is not actually at fault. However, scapegoating is also described as a rational act because it then allows a community to continue functioning through collective absolution. The scapegoat takes the blame for some sins that the community cannot or will not reconcile.

The function of COVID-19 blame-shifting

Before vaccines were readily available, some 25,000 people died from COVID-19 in Canada. Thousands of vulnerable older adults died in nursing homes, racialized communities bore a disproportionate share of death and suffering, people experiencing homelessness did not receive the support or care they needed to stay healthy and survive, and many others were left to fend for themselves.

At the federal and provincial levels, governments failed to make good decisions concerning public health, and failed to learn lessons and made the same mistakes repeatedly. Canadian governments engaged in vaccine nationalism, among the worst actors of any developed countries, while in the public sphere, a discussion took place about whether the country was at "the front of the line." And unfortunately, it has to be said that lots of individuals did not do their part either. I am not going into detail on this here, other than to say that while tens of thousands of people died, many people insisted on their holidays and creature comforts.

The point is, ugly things happened during the pandemic in Canada. Most of this ugliness is not something people want to talk about and is actually something people want to cover over and forget. When much of the country got vaccinated in 2021, it provided an opportunity to start fresh. It was a chance to purge the guilt from our collective psyche. All the bad behaviour, the unnecessary suffering and death, all of it was magically erased for anyone who got a syringe of vaccine injected in their arm.[2] Those who would not get vaccinated, of course, then became solely responsible for all the ugliness that came before.

In this way, the unvaccinated are a convenient and easy target for those politicians who are unwilling to accept any responsibility for the failures of their leadership and the role their decisions played in the collapse of the healthcare system. And the unvaccinated are a convenient target for a public that wants to absolve itself of sin for the many and egregious transgressions they would rather forget.

It is irrational and rational at the same time. Irrational, in the sense that anti-vaccine protesters are not in any way responsible for the ugliness that played out in this country during the first year-and-a-half of the pandemic. Rational, in the sense that the caricature of the anti-vax protester is a convenient vessel for the deep-seated guilt so many are keen to forget. Like any scapegoat, all the sins are placed upon them, and they are cast out of the community so that everyone else can move on.

---

[2] There is something to be said, in my view, of the mass vaccination campaign serving as a religious experience, with adherents being reborn and washed clean, as in a baptism or other such ceremony of absolution and redemption. This may be an interesting subject for a dissertation by an enterprising religious studies scholar.

Canada's COVID reckoning

To be clear, once again, none of this is meant to justify protests in front of hospitals by anti-vaccine protesters or to generate any sympathy for their cause. I disagree with them, and I feel that if they want to claim their right not to get vaccinated, they also need to accept their responsibility not to endanger the rest of the community. But the rest of the community also needs to accept its responsibility. Getting vaccinated does not absolve people of their responsibility for what happened. And as a whole, the country will need to come to a serious reckoning if we ever hope to move past this collective failure and collective shame. That reckoning cannot happen when the first impulse is to simply scapegoat anti-vaxxers and to avoid the truth of the situation.

Understanding COVID-19 anti-vaccine and anti-mandate protests

Engaging anti-vaccine and anti-mandate sentiment on its own terms disrupts the caricature of the unvaccinated

Stating clearly and upfront: I am not advocating anti-vaccine and anti-mandate positions and I do not sympathize with the cause.[1] However, as with any protest movement, it is important to attempt to understand what it means and how it functions for the people who are on the inside. People who take part in protest movements for the most part believe in what they are doing, or at least that it is something they should do even if they do not believe in the cause absolutely, and see their movement as legitimate. Any analysis attempting to genuinely understand a movement must begin from that same place, and be able to argue the positions of the movement as well as or better than its adherents, if only to then be able to more effectively argue against such positions.

---

[1] This chapter is based on a strategy paper I wrote in September 2021, and that was subsequently expanded and revised in light of intensification of anti-vaccine and anti-mandate protests in the first few months of 2022, the so-called freedom convoys or trucker protests.

It is also helpful to understand what the protest movement may be doing for those who are outside of it within the broader public and the protest's function in society as a whole.[2] In many cases, for example, a protest movement can be a convenient way of promoting a political agenda, either by showing support for or by denouncing a movement. Protest movements can also be used as scapegoats, for example like what in Orwell's *1984* was the function of the "five-minute hate." In this way, a protest movement can help to create a collective identity by defining what that identity opposes. This may then have a knock-on effect of reinforcing the sense of collective identity or persecution within a movement, such as by proving to movement insiders that the broader society is unwilling to even consider what are to insiders thought of as their legitimate concerns.

It needs to be said, as well, that not all protest movements and organizers intend to build mass movements or subscribe to a theory of political change that assumes massive numbers of participants is what will shift a given policy or further some specific goals. Many outsiders will imagine that the point of any protest is to convince them, or others like them, to change over to some different point of view. But there are theories of political change that do not assume massive public involvement, and there is almost always a wide range of views within movements about how goals can or should be accomplished. For example, the anti-vaccine movement is quite old, and the protests around the COVID-19 pandemic are just the latest chapter in its evolution. Movement insiders may see the current pandemic as simply an opportunity to recruit future leaders or devotees, and not as the endgame as such. For some organizers, it may be

---

[2] For more on the function of protest movements for outsiders or for the broader society, see the earlier chapter, "Anti-vaccine protests and blame-shifting COVID-19 ethical responsibility in Canada," which discusses the unvaccinated as a convenient scapegoat.

more important to recruit one new fundamentalist follower while alienating a wide swath of the public. Now, that is not to say that in the current anti-vaccine and anti-mandate protests that there is no intent to bring large numbers of people into the movement. Just that there are always many different goals and that, as outsiders, people should not assume that the message is always directed at them.

The most obvious source of contention leading to these anti-vaccine and anti-mandate protests is the direct loss of income and opportunities for those who refuse to get a vaccine. But while these protests were sparked by issues around vaccines, part of what motivates significant numbers of people involved is rooted in pre-existing or underlying grievances. This is true of most any protest movement. There are long-standing grievances in Canada around jobs, the cost of living, health care, rights and civil liberties, and many other legitimate grievances. Moreover, many participants have a deep distrust of governments of all kinds, once again often for perfectly legitimate reasons. While specific issues like vaccinations and mandates may be the spark that started this protest movement, this upsurge of social unrest is happening because of specific conditions to do with the everyday lives of people. No protest movement ever just starts from nowhere. There is always some groundwork that was laid months, years, or decades before.

For example, the last thirty or forty years of what is often called neoliberalism has seen the hollowing out of industry and manufacturing, with many companies and jobs being exported to countries with lower costs of labour and less regulation or taxes.[3] At the same time, wealth has been accumulating into the hands of a small number of people alongside a huge increase in

---

[3] David Harvey, *A Brief History of Neoliberalism*, Oxford University Press, 2007.

inequality in Canada. It is also arguably the case that some rights and freedoms are under attack. Successive Canadian federal governments have encroached on civil liberties, such as laws that criminalize forms of protest and allow the security services to trample on press freedoms. The expansion of the state's surveillance capacities that encroach on privacy is also a concern. Some of these concerns around the economy, rights, and freedoms are part of groundwork for, and directly feed into, the concerns of the anti-vaccine and anti-mandate protests. It is important to see the actual vaccines and mandates as only a part of what motivates participants to get involved. There is a broader context for these protests.

Even people whose main concerns are vaccines or mandates are not all the same. Some promote naturopathy, allopathy, or other nonmedical approaches. Some are right-wing libertarians who believe government is tyrannical and using the pandemic as cover to extinguish rights. There are left-wingers who claim pharmaceutical companies are taking advantage for profit. There are authoritarians, anti-authoritarians, conspiracy theorists, religious fundamentalists, and people who have simply fallen for propaganda. There are even outright fascists who see the protests as a vehicle to spread their odious and dangerous ideas. In this sense, the protests can be broadly defined as a form of populism in that they are many things to many people.

It is also worth considering that those who put themselves forward as organizers within anti-vaccine and anti-mandate movements may have less-than-obvious reasons for what they are doing. For some of the central organizers of these protests, at least in Canada, anti-vaccine and anti-mandate sentiments appears to be only one part of a spectrum of fringe or extremist views, and it is rare to find an organizer who is only interested in the issue at hand. Many of the key voices are enamoured, or at least pretend to be enamoured, with conspiratorial ideas. On a basic level, key organizers may not be involved because they necessarily believe in the cause they are organizing around. Some organizers may at times be working with a different end in mind than the current issue at hand, or simply be opportunists.

In short, to understand a protest movement, one must first set out to authentically engage with the many diverse motives of those involved and think through the ways the movement functions, for both insiders and outsiders. Its arguments, no matter how outlandish they seem, must be seen as a legitimate position from their point of view, and its concerns need to be taken seriously, rather than falling into a view of the world as consisting simply of "good guys and bad guys."

The unvaccinated and social justice

It is important to pause here for a moment and mention, before discussing the history of the anti-vaccine movement, that there is a social justice element to vaccination, and it is necessary to take this into account in discussions related to the politics of vaccinations in Canada. Black and Indigenous people are overrepresented in vaccine hesitancy and among unvaccinated populations.[4] Black and Indigenous people have higher than average COVID-19 case rates, hospitalizations, and deaths. People with disabilities also make up a significant part of unvaccinated populations, either because the vaccine itself poses a risk to their health or because they cannot mount an effective immune response.[5] People with disabilities are also

---

[4] For more on the relevant data and history of this issue, see the Statistics Canada report, "COVID-19 vaccine willingness among Canadian population groups," August 20, 2021; and Azza Eissa et al., "Increasing SARS-CoV-2 vaccination rates among Black people in Canada," *CMAJ*, August 9, 2021

[5] Sara Rotenberg et al., "COVID-19 vaccination for people with disabilities," Ontario COVID-19 Science Advisory Table, June 8, 2021;

overrepresented in COVID-19 infection rates, hospitalizations, and deaths.

Vaccine hesitancy among Black and Indigenous communities is rooted in histories of colonialism, racism, and documented medical experimentation.[6] This is not something that happened in the distant past. Residential school survivors still alive today recall being used as test subjects for vaccines and other medical treatments. The Tuskegee study, which was a U.S. Public Health Service research project that ran until 1972 and did not collect informed consent of participants, is one of several flashpoints for vaccine hesitancy among Black people.[7] Along with historical perspectives, present-day realities of inequality, lack of access to health care, homelessness, criminalization, and numerous other social and economic factors disproportionately affect Black and Indigenous people and lead to worse outcomes with COVID-19.

Vaccine hesitancy and anti-vaccine sentiment is, in this way, as much an issue of social justice as it is a medical issue for some people in Black and Indigenous communities. This is not a view that is typically brought up in reporting or news about anti-vaccine or anti-mandate sentiment, which all too often is more in line with scapegoating or caricaturing than with actually explaining why such sentiment exists. Acknowledging any part of that history and present-day reality puts an altogether sinister tone to the types of rhetoric circulating

---

and WHO and UNICEF policy brief, "Disability considerations for COVID-19 vaccination," April 19, 2021.

[6] Ian Mosby and Jaris Swidrovich, "Medical experimentation and the roots of COVID-19 vaccine hesitancy among Indigenous Peoples in Canada," *CMAJ*, March 15, 2021; and Michele L. Norris, "Black people are justifiably wary of a vaccine," *Washington Post*, December 9, 2020.

[7] "The U.S. Public Health Service syphilis study at Tuskegee" on the Center for Disease Control website, April 22, 2021.

about how the so-called anti-vaxxers and the unvaccinated should be treated, such as the commonly repeated notion that they should be denied medical care and left to die.

People with disabilities are also grappling with issues of social justice related to the pandemic. Many disability advocates and activists have, throughout the pandemic, raised issues around how their perspectives were neglected by policy makers.[8] There is also a recent history of eugenics and other disturbing views on the disposability of anyone who does not fit within some narrow set of characteristics for paradigm citizenship.[9] People with disabilities, like other marginalized groups, are disproportionately affected by some of the worst outcomes of COVID-19, whether that is with infections, hospitalizations, or death rates. While COVID-19 and vaccines are medical issues, for people with disabilities they are also social justice issues, in the sense that ongoing injustices are a factor and contribute to worse outcomes.

I am not raising this issue of social justice and vaccinations to say that people with disabilities or Black and Indigenous people are centrally involved in anti-vaccine and anti-mandate protests. In fact, from what can be gained in observational and anecdotal evidence, the protesters are primarily made up of the so-called paradigm citizens of this country, i.e., white and able-bodied. I raise this point of vaccines and social justice,

---

[8] Laura Mullins and Maureen Connolly, "Voices lost in crisis: Adults with IDD share their lived experience during the COVID-19 pandemic," Brock University, September 2021; and Mouhamad Rachini, Alison Masemann, and Meli Gumus, "As restrictions loosen up, advocates for people with disabilities say their needs haven't been considered," *The Current*, February 10, 2022.

[9] Lennard Davis, "In the time of pandemic, the deep structure of biopower is laid bare," *Critical Inquiry 47*, 2021; and Jacqueline Fox, "The current COVID-19 surge, eugenics, and health-based discrimination," *Bill of Health*, July 23, 2021.

rather, to further highlight and disrupt the caricature of unvaccinated people and of anti-vaccine sentiment. I discuss some of the history of the anti-vaccine movement below, and similar points come up for the movement as a whole, though I did want to specifically highlight this issue of social justice first and on its own, since it is all too often unacknowledged.

Brief history of the anti-vaccine movement

The anti-vaccine movement emerged at almost the same time vaccinations became widespread as a way to prevent diseases.[10] The first modern vaccine was created by Edward Jenner in 1796 to fight smallpox, though there is evidence of similar techniques of using infected tissue to create immunity against infectious diseases, including as early as 1000 CE in China.[11] Earlier vaccines of the type used by Jenner were not as safe as those available today, but they still did the job they were designed to do, which was to protect against major infectious diseases that harried communities all over the world, including smallpox, measles, and polio. However, many people did not trust the governments and health agencies that came to them with vaccination campaigns, and were especially wary when it came to vaccinations for their children.[12] There is a natural and fundamental protective instinct when it comes to taking any chances with the health of children, and although vaccines are

---

[10] Bernice L. Hausman, *Anti/Vax: Reframing the Vaccination Controversy*, ILR Press, 2019.

[11] "History of Vaccines," College of Physicians of Philadelphia.

[12] Even with COVID-19 vaccines, the uptake among children, and by proxy the willingness of parents to have their children vaccinated, has been underwhelming in Canada. As of March 2022, only some 25% of eligible children between the ages of five and eleven had been fully vaccinated, even though there is ample supply and vaccination has been open for this age group since November 2021. Children are, therefore, a large part of the unvaccinated, which once again shows that the unvaccinated are not quite as they are caricatured.

by definition far safer than the diseases they fight against, it is understandable that even those parents who themselves get vaccinated would hesitate when it comes to their kids.

One of the reasons for early skepticism about vaccines, even with serious infectious diseases like smallpox, which killed one in four people infected, included complications caused by unsanitary vaccination clinics or administration. There were also serious cases of contaminated batches of vaccine, which in some extreme examples caused hundreds of deaths. One particularly troubling case was a tuberculosis vaccine that was administered in a German town in the late 1920s that caused the deaths of 72 infants.[13] The reason for the tragedy was that the same lab that was manufacturing the vaccines was studying a strain of tuberculosis and contaminated the batch with the virus. This and other issues of contamination or harms caused by the vaccines or by the vaccine campaigns led some to conclude that the vaccine was more dangerous than the disease it was supposed to prevent. Commentators point out that when things go wrong in vaccination, the damage to public confidence can be difficult to overcome.[14] Many more people may die if they are not vaccinated, but deaths caused by the vaccines themselves are perceived to be more egregious.[15]

---

[13] Gregory J. Fox, Marianna Orlova, and Erwin Schurr, "Tuberculosis in newborns: The lessons of the 'Lübeck Disaster' (1929-1933)" *PLOS Pathogens 12.1, 2016.*

[14] Hausman, *Anti/Vax: Reframing the Vaccination Controversy.*

[15] Likewise with present-day COVID-19 vaccines, which are proven to be far safer than the disease itself, there have been some instances of serious side effects and deaths in people of all ages. One major issue in Canada was the use of the AstraZeneca vaccine, which faced issues around blood clots and was eventually discontinued. The COVID-19 vaccinations were initially happening in an emergency situation, with research essentially happening while the doses were administered. Any harms caused by the vaccines or any changes of policy were quickly seized upon by the anti-vaccine movement as proof of both the dangers and irrelevancy of vaccination.

Historically, there has also been a class element to vaccine hesitancy and in the genesis of early anti-vaccine movements. In the broadest sense, working-class people doubted the motives of the upper-class authorities who presumed to be their benefactors, since all too often those same authorities did nothing but visit misery on them.[16] People were forced into unsafe workplaces and could be conscripted into militaries, and it was not uncommon for working-class people to suspect that the upper classes viewed them as simply human resources to be deployed, sacrificed, and managed. In the context of widespread class antagonisms and revolutions throughout the 19th and 20th centuries, vaccination campaigns could easily be perceived as simply another attempt by the upper class to control the bodies of the working class. Alongside class, sectarianism and ethnic tensions could also play a part, as was the case in Montreal in the late-1800s, when French-Catholics distrusted the Anglo-Protestant doctors who were trying to administer smallpox vaccines. The incident ended in a major civil disturbance and rioting.[17]

Various types of vaccine mandates and health orders have also been a serious source of contention, historically and up to the present.[18] There have been numerous incidents of people and of whole communities being vaccinated forcefully or otherwise being compelled to get vaccinated under threat of force. A basic premise of the anti-vaccine movement has all along been bodily autonomy, both of the individual and of their

---

[16] Nadja Durbach, "'They might as well brand us': Working-class resistance to compulsory vaccination in Victorian England," *Social History of Medicine* 13.1, 2000.

[17] Jonathan M. Berman, "When antivaccine sentiment turned violent: The Montréal Vaccine Riot of 1885," *CMAJ* 193.14, April 6, 2021.

[18] Indeed, throughout the history of the anti-vaccine movement, mandates themselves have been the main source of contention rather than the vaccines.

children.[19] Vaccine mandates have also been opposed based on religious grounds, such as among religions or religious sects who oppose anything that can be seen as tampering with the so-called natural human being. In Canada, the Vaccination Act of 1887 was among the first explicit vaccine mandates. It was immediately met by the creation of the Canadian Anti-Vaccination League, which started that same year and was modelled on similar anti-vaccination organizations in the United Kingdom and the United States.[20] It is interesting to note that these organizations generally pop up in response to vaccine mandates, rather than in response to the vaccines themselves, showing that the issue is as much about choice and bodily autonomy as it is about the vaccine or any issues around safety. In short, they do not oppose the vaccines, so long as they are not forced to get them. Generally, it is helpful to think that the main objections to vaccination are social or political objections to mandates, and not medical or scientific objections per se.[21] Still, such organizations did often engage with medical or scientific information, and at times even spread their own purposeful misinformation, to meet their goals of opposing mandates.

Anti-vaccination movements and organizations have seen their support go up and down, depending on factors to do with the social, political, cultural, or economic tides. Like many long-lived movements, it is best understood as opportunistic,

---

[19] Even with COVID-19 vaccine mandates, which were enacted for some workplaces, educational settings, or transportation, governments stopped short of mandating vaccination for children to attend public schools.

[20] There have been dozens of other such anti-vaccination groups in Canada. One of the most prominent today is Vaccine Choice Canada. The group spreads misinformation including that vaccines can cause autism. The group carried out a major campaign throughout the COVID-19 pandemic, latching onto various issues as they came up.

[21] Ellen Amster, "Why is anyone anti-vaccine? A history of vaccination and anti-vaccination," McMaster University, 2015.

ready to take advantage when the moment is right, and ready to try to maintain itself when things are less than optimal. Outbreaks of infectious disease, and especially those that prompt vaccine mandates by authorities, such as previous measles, smallpox, tuberculosis, and other outbreaks, are often seen as an opportunity to grow and bring new people into the fold. The current COVID-19 pandemic is no different. Leaders within the movement can be understood as being opportunistic as well. In many cases, when issues around vaccination come to the fore, grifters or what were previously called snake oil salesmen tried to take advantage of the situation for their own financial gain. These may be people with no affinity for the social or political issues of the movement, but simply recognize that situations of panic and uncertainty can be profitable. Even those leaders within the movement who do have a true ideological affinity may also be willing to spread misinformation or stir up panic in the public, justifying the tactic with the assumption that the end justifies the means.[22] Studies have shown, in the COVID-19 era, that online misinformation has been a major source of vaccine hesitancy and of anti-vaccine and anti-mandate sentiment.[23] Such forms of opportunism by anti-vaccination groups and of movement leaders, actual or pretend, need to be seen as factors in historical and present-day upsurges of vaccine hesitancy.

Beyond the caricature

The anti-vaccine and anti-mandate movements have more complexity than the simplistic caricature presented in most media reports. A more fulsome account of such movements

---

[22] Tara Haelle, "This is the moment the anti-vaccine movement has been waiting for," *New York Times*, August 31, 2021.

[23] Renee Garett and Sean Young, "Online misinformation and vaccine hesitancy," *Translational Behavioral Medicine* 11.12, 2021.

must include an awareness of the social justice issues and the historical context. All the issues around safety, social class, ethnicity, moral and political objections, and the opportunism of the organizations and their leaders are only a sample of the many complex and intersecting influences on the anti-vaccine and anti-mandate movements. In the COVID-19 pandemic and the ongoing vaccination campaigns, there is also, for example, even an issue of geopolitics to consider, in the sense that various state actors have an interest in vaccinating their own populations and also potentially in stirring up protests and discontent in other states. It is not, in short, just an issue that can be easily reduced to "good guys and bad guys."

Once again, however, what I am not saying is that anyone needs to support such views. It is helpful and important, in my view, to be able to authentically engage with and to take seriously the anti-vaccine and anti-mandate movements and the protests they create. But that analysis is intended to allow for more robust refutation of their arguments and claims. And since those claims are so often based on social and political considerations, and not, for most people in the movements, based on scientific or medical issues, the most effective counter-arguments will be those based on ethics and social solidarity. After all, even though there are a number of legitimate concerns in the movement, those concerns are outweighed by the responsibility to contribute to the health and well-being of our communities and of society as a whole.

That said, it is also my view that personal choice, autonomy, and consent need to be primary. There should be no use of force or threat to compel anyone to get vaccinated. But those who make a choice and exercise their autonomy must also respect those around them and the choices they make. In short, anyone should be allowed to refuse a vaccine, but their right to choose does not mean they can endanger others. They should have the decency to not impose on those who do not impose on them. If they do not, then any community can take steps to exclude those who choose not to live up to their responsibilities. No moral person accepts rights but refuses the responsibilities that go along with those rights.

In the end, the caricature of the unvaccinated is not helpful for learning how to most effectively deal with anti-vaccine and anti-mandate sentiment. The true picture of the unvaccinated that emerges is something much less clear-cut than what is commonly presented in media reports. As with many social and political movements, there are interests at play, and various stakeholders vying for position and advantage. Any engagement with anti-vaccine and anti-mandate movements or protests will benefit from carefully analyzing and authentically considering their arguments. A failure to do so may result in unintended consequences or risk enflaming the situation further.

Learning to live (and die) with it

Saying we must learn to live with COVID-19 without a plan for how to do so is simply capitulation

Here at the beginning of 2022, as the Omicron wave continues to batter communities throughout Canada, politicians and bosses of all stripes have taken up the defeatist epitaph, "we need to learn to live with it."[1]

It is a phrase that is at once extraordinarily potent and also supremely absurd. It creates the conditions for its own truth, in the sense that accepting the supposed inevitability of widespread transmission of the virus and the disease it causes means there is no choice but to learn to live with it. It is a phrase that gaslights anyone who has attempted to avoid becoming infected and avoid transmitting the virus on to others for the past two years, since now it is a given that "everyone will get it," as they say. It is easy to wonder, why did we even bother trying for so long? It is a phrase that indicates bowing to that base element who have all along used similarly dismissive rhetoric: "the cure is worse than the disease"; "stop living in fear"; "it ends when we stop believing in it." It vindicates the irresponsible. It is being used not only by public figures, but also

---

[1] Published in *The Independent NL*, January 28, 2022.

by bosses and managers to dismiss employees' concerns about returning to work in the context of widespread community transmission, as though workers have some irrational fear of "the sniffles."[2]

Begging the question

But it is also a phrase that has a blistering critique embedded within it, if we are able get past the feeling of dejection it first conjures. "We have to learn to live with it," they say. Then tell us how?

Learning to live with it has to be more than just giving up and pretending life can go back to the way it was before 2020, as if by some sort of magic. If we are going to learn to live with it, then we need to create the conditions so that can actually happen. Otherwise, as we've seen over and over again throughout the pandemic, there'll just be another variant or wave of infection lurking around the corner that will swamp the healthcare system and force the country into more lockdowns.

If the virus is here to stay, we need an actual plan and actual policies that will allow us to hold the worst effects at bay. It cannot just be hygiene theatre and it certainly cannot just be hand-waving and magical thinking. What is the plan to keep transmission of the virus to what are called manageable levels? What policies are being put in place to look after the most vulnerable people in society? What is the proposal to actually make schools safe for children? How will workplaces be regulated and required to provide protections for workers? What supports are in place for the vast number of people who have

---

[2] As I note later in the chapter "The pandemic and social relations," it is perfectly rational for workers, having witnessed the way so many were made disposable throughout the pandemic, to wonder if the bosses and leaders of the world might not truly have their health and well-being in mind in their zeal to reopen workplaces.

become disabled because of COVID? If there are not any clear answers to these and other simple questions of policy, then it is not learning to live with it. It is capitulation and learning to die with it.

Gross negligence

It is an astonishing dereliction of duty for those in positions of power to just throw up their hands, allow the virus to rip through the population, and say "learn to live with it." These are people who claim the right to make decisions on our behalf based on the premise that they have our best interests and our well-being in mind.

Forget for a moment that there is absolutely no need to swing the gates wide open during the biggest wave of infections, when waiting even weeks for reopening is just simple prudence.[3] Governments and organizations of all kinds have had two years to get their acts together. They had two years to figure out best practices for protecting kids in schools, workers in workplaces, vulnerable people in care settings, and generally to sort out some set of social conventions to allow people to live and work in the midst of the virus.

Saying we must learn to live with it while having no plan whatsoever for how to do that undermines the legitimacy of those in positions of authority, and the phrase is, in the end, simply code for "we give up" and "you are on your own." If any of us was assigned an important project and after two years came back with only irrelevancy and window-dressing, we would surely be fired.

---

[3] The Omicron wave of the pandemic, which started in December 2021 in Canada, involved a highly transmissible variant and infected more people in a few months than had been infected throughout the whole of the COVID-19 pandemic up to that point.

The saying goes that when someone shows you who they are you should believe them. And in this case, what we are being shown is that a lot of people in positions of authority just do not want to do their jobs. It shows that it is well past time for us to have a candid conversation about who it is we have in charge, and whose interests they really serve.

The pandemic and social relations

Long-lasting impact of the pandemic on interpersonal relationships may be the worst effect of all

The first thing that should come to mind when thinking about the costs of the COVID-19 pandemic is the immediate human tragedy.[1] The human costs in Canada can be counted in the 35,000 deaths, the millions of people who were infected, some of whose health will never be the same, and the more general damage to the mental health and well-being of millions more. After that, costs could be counted in the economic impacts of lockdowns, unemployment and livelihoods lost, as well as the massive increases of public debt.

However, one of the biggest costs that no one is counting is the destroyed interpersonal relationships, such as relationships in families, between friends, among coworkers, and even more generally all the connections between people that make up our society. As the sociologists tell us, society is precisely this set of relationships that exist between people. These kinds of simple and everyday social relations are the basis for everything else that we do economically, politically, and culturally.

---

[1] Published in *The Independent NL*, February 10, 2022.

When social relations break down, everything else people rely upon and take for granted is prone to breaking down as well.

The damage to individual social relations

The damage that has been done to social relations through the pandemic comes in a few different forms, which are more or less obvious. Some of the obvious forms of frayed relationships are due to the politicization and polarization that is happening because of anti-vaccine and anti-mandate sentiment.

In recent weeks here in Canada, for example, this sentiment has been expressed in protests and blockades, but the same discontent has been with us since the very earliest days of the pandemic.[2] Polarization is also happening across the political spectrum, with greater distinctions being drawn between the mainstream political parties on pandemic-related topics. Such issues are enough to strain many relationships, and people find it hard to accept their friends or family members subscribe to particular views. Some are even cutting people out of their lives because the disagreements run so deep.[3] Even when relationships are not fully broken, friends and families may not be able to talk about such issues, if they can even stand to be around each other.

More generally, relationships can also be strained because of particular kinds of behaviours throughout the pandemic. It has been difficult to navigate socializing of any kind, and this can easily be a source of tension. For example, people may feel

---

[2] In February 2022, anti-vaccine and anti-mandate protests set up occupations in Ottawa and other Canadian cities. This series of protests was an intensification of the existing pandemic-related unrest. See the chapter above, "A wave of mass social unrest lies on the horizon," which was written in April 2020 and describes some of the earliest anti-lockdown protests.

[3] Mark Gollom, "People are severing friendships over convoy protest, with some saying it shows 'true colours,'" *CBC*, February 5, 2022.

that their family or friends are acting inappropriately in the context of a public health emergency.[4] The flip side of that coin is that people may also feel their friends or family are acting morally superior or overly cautious.

Whether it is brash acts of protest or simple tensions over socializing, the damage can be permanent, and many people will be unable to think of their family members or friends as they did before.

The damage to social cohesion

Political polarization or strained relationships are in many ways obvious compared with other strained social relations. We can actually see demonstrations in the streets, recognize the divide opening up between segments of the population, and feel the frayed relationships with friends and family. The more difficult thing to deal with for many is the harsh realization that those around them – society as a whole – did not value their existence. The community that was supposed to be a support network did not care if people lived or died. This is a somewhat more amorphous form of the breakdown of social relations, and it is perhaps better understood as the undermining of social co-hesion.

As an aside, I should mention that the breakdown of social cohesion or the feeling of general social callousness was not necessarily uniform across the country. Some provinces, like my home province of Newfoundland and Labrador, arguably had the kinds of social solidarity and social cohesion that would have made a big difference in other parts of the country.

---

[4] See the above chapter, "Why are so many not following COVID-19 guidelines?" for a discussion and analysis of how never having been on the receiving end of social solidarity makes people ill-equipped to enact it.

Some of the simplest expressions of the generalized social callousness involved those who acted in ways that did not take into consideration the safety and well-being of those around them. This is a widespread and general sentiment that many people felt. However, the breakdown of social cohesion is a feeling that is especially pronounced among people with disabilities and among older adults. Many people with disabilities, for example, long suspected they were considered disposable, even before the pandemic, but now know they could just die and no one would care. And in fact, some people would be relieved.[5] Older adults have also been treated as disposable. Data tracking by Nora Loreto shows 19,807 of 34,538 recorded pandemic deaths were in residential care facilities, most of which were older adults.[6]

Much of the death and suffering happened away from the public view, and there has been little effort to reconcile or mourn this national tragedy. Still, many people do recognize what has happened, and also recognize it could as easily have been them, since we will all, if we live long enough, become old and disabled. The realization that anyone could simply be cast on the trash pile cannot help but damage social relations and

---

[5] Rochelle Walensky, the director of the U.S. Center for Disease Control, made the statement that she found it "encouraging" that it was mostly people with multiple "comorbidities" who were dying of COVID during the Omicron wave. Her statement was immediately and roundly condemned by disability activists and disability advocacy groups, who pointed out the term comorbidities is essentially used as a byword for disabled, and that the statement amounted to a tacit acknowledgement of the disposability of people with disabilities. See Susan Henderson, "DREDF's open letter to CDC and director Rochelle P. Walensky," Disability Rights Education & Defense Fund, January 9, 2022.

[6] See Nora Loreto's publicly available online spreadsheet, "Deaths in residential care in Canada by facility," which she has been compiling throughout the pandemic.

cohesion in a society like ours, that claims to hold compassion and humanitarianism as core values.

Where we go from here

Taking into account the breakdown of social relations and the long catalogue of ethical failures throughout the COVID-19 pandemic in Canada, it is easy to imagine that this country is in for a difficult post-pandemic era, whenever that may arrive.[7] Even now, as much of the country attempts to reopen once again, the fraying of social relations is having an impact.

Is it any wonder that so many people are not keen to go back to "normal" after having seen the way this society makes people disposable and throws them away? Is it at all surprising they might not want to go back to their workplaces amidst an ongoing pandemic wave and might not trust that those who claim to be leaders truly have their well-being in mind? How can thoughtful people feel good about going back into a society that has a set of bared fangs?

Before the pandemic people believed, at least on some level, that those around them had their back and if push came to shove their family, friends, and the community as a whole would stand up and do the right thing. Now, many will never be able to think about their family or friends the same way and they will never feel part of a community.

What cost can be put on that?

---

[7] For discussion of these ethical failures, see the above chapters "The failure of common decency" and "What explains the Canadian failure on COVID-19?"

The freedom to be equally indecent as everyone else

*Anti-mandate protests are unethical,
but so is the rest of Canada's COVID-19 response*

It is easy to see the selfishness of the so-called freedom convoy protests.[1] Here is a group of people essentially demanding to be allowed to endanger others and perpetuate the pandemic. Make no mistake, these are protests on behalf of the virus. However, an uncomfortable thing to do is to take seriously the rationale for the protests. Being unvaccinated means that you can become infected and then transmit the virus. But that is true, in the Omicron wave, if you are vaccinated as well.

So the question is, why should unvaccinated people be prohibited from going around infecting others if vaccinated people are free to do so?

I know it may seem disingenuous to put it that way because unvaccinated people account for a disproportionate share of burden on the healthcare system and cause a disproportionate part of the problem. I do understand there are real differences here. The point, though, is that these protests are actually about freedom: the freedom to be equally indecent as everyone else.

---

[1] Previously unpublished chapter written in early February 2022.

Looking in the mirror

Think about what is currently happening in Ontario, where the provincial government has hastily thrown open the barn doors once again. Employers are bringing workers back to the office, restaurants and gyms are open, and everything is full speed ahead. These decisions are prolonging the Omicron wave, and leading to ongoing infection, hospitalizations, and deaths, when waiting a couple of weeks would have made reopening much safer.

The justification is that in this wave fewer people are being hospitalized and dying as a percentage of total infections. Or, as the director of the U.S. Center for Disease Control put it, it is "encouraging" that only certain types of people are dying — that is, those with so-called "comorbidities."[2] But remember that the Ontario government hastily reopened in each of the preceding waves, too. And so did governments all across Canada, with a few notable exceptions. Those decisions were taken on behalf of the public and led to thousands of unnecessary deaths. Since the start of the pandemic, some 35,000 people have died, of whom some 20,000 were people in residential care settings. For the most part, these were vulnerable older adults and people with disabilities.

Remember, as well, the majority of those deaths happened before there was any widespread availability of vaccines, so we cannot blame the unvaccinated for that. In fact, we did know the kinds of things to do in order to prevent waves of infection and death, but found it inconvenient at Christmas or when it was time to go on that late-winter getaway.[3]

---

[2] Susan Henderson, "DREDF's open letter to CDC and director Rochelle P. Walensky," Disability Rights Education & Defense Fund, January 9, 2022.

[3] Here, I am thinking of the way the Ontario government neglected to put restrictions in place until after the Christmas holidays in 2021.

People in glass houses

Just to say, it is easy to find glaring and recurrent examples of indecency throughout the pandemic in Canada. Even now, the cavalier way that governments and organizations of all kinds have reopened is just more callousness directed toward people with disabilities and other vulnerable people, who have all along been crying out for even the slightest recognition of their plight.

On the individual level, many vaccinated people act as though getting a shot in the arm cleansed them of all sin, as if they waded in the holy waters of Lourdes. And as they go back to the mall or out to brunch, they find a convenient scapegoat in the unvaccinated, who are now somehow solely responsible for all that is wrong in society.

Is that a little bit harsh? Sure. But if we want to undermine the selfish and unethical demands of anti-mandate protesters, it would probably help to be standing on firm ethical grounds.

COVID-19 and the unravelling of Canadian identity

Canada's failed pandemic response further undermines foundational ideas of the country

Canadian identity does a lot of heavy lifting in this country.[1] It holds people together stretched across a vast geography. It props up politics, economics, and culture. In a significant way, it makes the country exist.

The term Canadian identity indicates the character, values, and aspirations of the nation. It is bound up with notions of humanitarianism, egalitarianism, and collective care. It is grounded in universal healthcare and peacekeeping, representative individuals like Terry Fox and Roberta Bondar, and cultural elements of Canadian arts, sport, and food. However, something to keep in mind about Canadian identity is that it is just an idea, a story we tell ourselves and others about who we are. It only exists because people believe it.

The country's response to the COVID-19 pandemic has made it more difficult for people to believe in Canadian identity and threatens to unravel the narrative altogether.

---

[1] Published in *The Independent NL*, March 1, 2022.

Catalogue of faults

It is not as though Canadian identity was uninterrupted before the pandemic. The country's colonial history and the ongoing oppression of Indigenous peoples disrupts idyllic notions of Canadian identity. Recent revelations of mass graves at residential school sites across the country made many people question their belief in Canadian identity.

Then there is the yawning inequality and growing poverty, run-away inflation pushing working people to the edge, an out-of-control housing market, and perpetually stagnant wages. These economic factors disrupt Canadian identity, too, in the sense that egalitarianism is shown to be a myth.

Now, with COVID-19, Canadian identity is reaching a breaking point. More than 35,000 people have died of COVID-19, with more than half that number being vulnerable older adults and people with disabilities. As though that was not bad enough, there are now some indications that the true number may be twice the official figure.[2]

The pandemic disproportionately affects racialized communities, in terms of infections, hospitalizations, and deaths, as well as with respect to vaccine inequity.[3] The politicians and decision-makers of all kinds repeatedly failed in the duty of care, choosing to prioritize economics over the lives and well-being of some of the most vulnerable people in the country.

On the community and household level, social relations have never been so strained in recent memory. Protesters picket hospitals, occupy major cities, and enforce armed blockades of strategic chokepoints. Provincial and federal governments work at odds, foreign influences connive and destabilize, and in

---

[2] Tara Moriarty et al., "Excess all-cause mortality during the COVID-19 epidemic in Canada," Royal Society of Canada, 2021.

[3] Francis Henry et al., *Impacts of COVID-19 on racialized communities*, Royal Society of Canada, 2021.

recent days the federal government invoked the Emergencies Act.[4] Who can look around, after two years of the pandemic, and see the vision of Canada they grew up believing in?

Going forward

Taking the original idea of what it means to be Canadian and laying it against the country as it is right now, the two pictures do not line up. There were already enough contradictions in the idea of Canadian identity, but now it is too much to hold together.

COVID-19 shattered Canada. The damage to social relations and to the idea of what it means to be Canadian may be the worst impacts of all because so much relies on those things that a huge vacuum is opening up in their absence. The country is entering a situation that is inherently unstable and dangerous.

Going forward, things do not look good. There are sure to be more difficulties around COVID-19, which it seems we have little capacity to address. Then there are all the other problems that the country faces – things like reconciliation, inequality, and climate change, which at present seem well beyond anything that could realistically be dealt with.

This is not just an academic concern, since Canadian identity has for so long provided unity and common purpose, along with the stability that brings. With that identity slipping away, the future of the country becomes troubled and uncertain.

---

[4] The Canadian federal government, under the leadership of Justin Trudeau, invoked the Emergencies Act, which replaced the old War Measures Act, on February 14, 2022, in response to ongoing unrest related to the so-called freedom convoy protests taking place across the country.

Conclusion

The most contentious claim of this book, at least concerning prevailing attitudes, is likely that Canada's response to the COVID-19 pandemic constitutes a failure of ethical action. The impulse to deny the failure, minimize it, or ignore the subject altogether is going to be overwhelming. Indeed, the political class will spin things in whatever way seems politically expedient, depending on whether a given politician is in government or opposition. There may be inquiries and committees formed, ostensibly to study shortcomings. While they may express sincere-sounding words of mourning for the dead and point to some structural problems in the healthcare system, they will ultimately stop short of assigning blame or labelling the country's COVID-19 response a failure. After making appropriate gestures of contrition, many official reports will likely celebrate what happened as some success of leadership and collective action.

Individually, many people will be eager to hear a message that vindicates their experiences of the pandemic as a time of difficulty and hardship, because it has been difficult for most people, and there has been plenty of hardship to go around. Many will want to forget about the tragedy and attempt to move on. Given the widespread grief, even if grief is unacknowledged, it is perfectly understandable that there will be little appetite to take stock of what has happened or think about the collective and individual failures of ethical action. Messages of success and heroic narratives of overcoming will be much more appealing.

But grief that is not acknowledged and not worked through always comes back. People will, I believe, know deep down that what has happened in this country is a failure, even if they are unable to admit it. The test of that, beyond any quantitative data, is they will not be able to hold their heads high. For who can deny that after two years of the COVID-19 pandemic, Canada is deeply wounded, filled with discontent, and with a difficult road ahead? There are countries whose people can look at their response to the pandemic so far and hold their heads high, and even in our own country, there are some regions where that is also the case. It is not simply a matter of counting the dead but of looking at how people either came together in the face of adversity or were shattered and fell apart.

Those few willing to acknowledge or engage with the failure of ethical action and the country's shortcomings after the first two years of the pandemic will also have to grapple with how to share the blame. Governments will be a popular target since the failure of leadership and duty of care is glaring. Other institutions and organizations will also come in for their share of the blame, especially those public and private organizations and companies that put profit ahead of the well-being of working people. It will not be surprising to see mass protests and waves of unrest for years to come. While economics will be part of what fuels unrest, another part will be the loss of legitimacy of those who presume to lead, make policy, and manage.

Beyond the failures of systems and organizations, people will also blame each other. Many will be unable to forgive or forget how people in their communities acted, just as many will be unable to move past what their friends and families did when ethical action was most needed. They may smile and pretend, but under the surface will flow a current of mistrust and resentment. Then, on the individual level, the tendency will be to find fault in others but to justify one's own actions as having caused no harm. However, as with collective grief, on an individual level, there will also be a crushing wave of self-debasement, which may be unacknowledged but will still gnaw at the conscience of thoughtful people. At the same time, there are also the challenges posed by the disintegration of everyday social relations and the loss of belief in community. Some of these challenges are already emerging, and more will surely come as the pandemic drags on. The disillusionment associated with the disruption of Canadian identity will be difficult for this country ever to overcome.

It is hard to imagine that Canada will deal adequately with the challenges still to come concerning COVID-19. Many are eager to announce the so-called acute phase of the pandemic is coming to an end, and an endemic stage is beginning. But that does not preclude recurring waves of infections and the appearance of new variants, which could be worse than those we have so far experienced. No matter how much people may wish it were so, the pandemic is not over. Pandemic fatigue, grief, and all the issues associated with a fragmented society will make it nearly impossible to do what is necessary in order to keep people safe in the years to come. Indeed, to say that COVID-19 is endemic is to say only some people will need to worry about it; that is, older adults, people with disabilities, or otherwise vulnerable people. From an ethical point of view, the so-called endemic phase may be the most brutal phase of the pandemic. It will show categorically just how many and just what type of people our society is willing to sacrifice in the name of "learning to live with it." Any other challenges beyond the pandemic – for example, the challenges posed by climate change or the challenges associated with reconciliation – seem well beyond our capacity to take seriously at present.

The question, then, is what to do about it. What can people do in the face of such an appalling failure of leadership, ethical action, and common decency? How do we move forward as individuals and as a country? Is it possible to salvage anything at all from Canada's experience of the pandemic? It is difficult to say for sure, and my cynicism and disappointment prevent me from ending with some positive affirmation of the essential goodness of this country and its people. But if we could take away the simple realization that rising to challenges is not just about data, available resources, and financial wealth, but about the values and ethics motivating action, that would be something. I am not sure it is a message Canadians will be eager to hear. Still, one of the best things that could happen right now would be a movement of principled ethical action aimed at a social, economic, and political transformation. It must sound extraordinarily naïve to say that because the reality is our society privileges the few ahead of the many, and that has perhaps been the major contributing factor in the failure of ethical action on COVID-19. In a situation like the one we face in Canada, ethical action is a form of resistance, and resistance is the only ethical option, even if there is little hope any good will come of it.

Acknowledgements

Thanks to Erika Steeves, for ongoing support of my work both as my editor and confidant, and for the expertise to bring this work from a jumbled series of articles to the finished product it is today.

Thanks to the editors at *Ricochet* and *The Independent NL* for the candid feedback and for publishing the original articles and essays. Much gratitude to Ethan Cox, Derrick O'Keefe, and Drew Brown. Special thanks to Robin Whitaker, who edited the "Beyond the crisis" series in *The Independent NL* and reminded me that sometimes what may appear to be a failure is actually the all-too-perfect working of a system doing precisely what it was designed to do.

Thanks also to Justin Brake, one of Canada's best and most principled journalists, whose council I value immensely, and to Srinivas Murthy, for helping me with any questions on infectious disease and for showing me what medical ethics is all about.

Finally, as always, thanks to the council and the commune. We keep trying and we keep going forward, ever with a sly smile.

About the author

Jon Parsons is a writer and researcher from Portugal Cove, NL. His journalism has appeared in *The Independent NL*, *Ricochet*, *The Tyee*, *CBC NL*, and other publications. He has published two other books, *Everyday Dissent: Politics and Resistance in Newfoundland and Labrador* (2016) and *Expressive Subjects* (2018), a workbook of creative writing prompts. Jon completed a PhD in English at Memorial University, researching in the fields of resistance studies and Newfoundland literature. He is a former community organizer, activist, and board member of Social Justice Co-operative NL.

www.jonparsons.ca

Manufactured by Amazon.ca
Bolton, ON